TWISTED PAIR

TWISTED PAIR

JACK MCGUIGAN

MCDOROBUSH & ASSOCIATES

The characters and events in this book are fictitious. Any similarity to real persons, living or dead, is coincidental and not intended by the author. Names, characters, and places are products of the author's imagination.

Copyright © 2024 by Jack McGuigan

All rights reserved. No part of this publication may be reproduced, distributed, or transmitted in any manner whatsoever without written permission except in the case of brief quotations embodied in news articles and reviews.

ISBN: 979-8-9909453-0-2

Printed in California

Book design by Maria Mayer Feng and Kate Ryan
for Studio Maria Mayer Feng, LLC.

To all telephone workers, past and present, who considered their efforts for excellent service a true mission.

twisted pair *n.* a type of communications cable, invented by Alexander Graham Bell, in which two conductors of a single circuit are twisted together to improve telephone lines reducing interference and crosstalk from other telephone lines

n. Two people who have the same or very similar thinking and actions that are generally viewed as crazy, dangerous, and violent

HEAD UNDER HEELS

Terry Simpson did not know that he was going to die today.

He liked Southern California when he was little. He was a native and always appreciated the weather. Only when he moved out to Seattle for a couple of years did he realize that he had taken California for granted. What began in Seattle during the first year of really appreciating "how green everything is" soon migrated to a thought that "it really rains here a lot" and finally morphed to "I've got to get out of here."

Although Terry missed the varied colors of leaves in Seattle, he soon found that green, yellow, and brown—the dominant color of leaves in Los Angeles, although boring and unremarkable—were a small price for what he now recognized as world-class climate.

Today was especially enjoyable, beyond the excellent weather. He was celebrating the fifth anniversary of his return to the telephone company. The contract between the union and the telephone company allowed previously employed employees to come back to the telephone company and connect their terms of service after 5 years—and enjoy any benefits the new addition of service totalled. His service got "bridged" (as telephone folks called it) to his previous thirteen years. Now with 18 years of service, he went from two weeks' annual vacation to four, and with the higher position on the seniority list, he could actually select the vacation dates he wanted. The Seattle experience was a move to a telecom start-up that was supposed to make him millions—it was more disappointing than the weather. Not only did he not make millions, but he'd depleted the savings he and his wife had cobbled together for years, because of the start-up's lower pay and ultimately worthless stock options. Luckily, he had kept his childhood home in Van Nuys when he moved to Seattle, but it needed repairs from tenants who evidently had multiple cats. It had taken quite some time to make his childhood home no longer smell like a litter box.

Alicia, his wife, had followed him north and then returned to California with him, but had harbored a low-grade bitterness about it. With the prospect of going to Hawaii in the summer, even she was letting go of the resentment of the move to Seattle. When she kissed him this morning, she promised Terry a "bridging celebration" tonight. He found himself smiling.

He'd surprised himself when he volunteered to take the trouble ticket.

"Hey man, I'm going to the Lakers tonight. I'm going to see the Black Mamba. Will you take this trouble ticket?" DeMarius had asked Terry in a manner of expectation that the answer would be "YES". Terry would normally require a "please" with a request like this, but was more distracted that DeMarius could get a ticket to the Kobe-led Lakers at all.

DeMarius Thomas was hired in the anti-gang initiative of the company, and Terry and most of the folks in the telephone garage thought he was an entitled jerk. But Terry was so joyful that day about the improvements in his vacation benefits that he would have said "YES" to anything. Plus, he wanted to meet someone who actually requested DeMarius. It was only a rare request that any customer requested a technician by name; the customer must have really liked the previous interaction with the technician. Why would anyone ever request to see DeMarius – especially again?

As he was approaching the address on the repair trouble ticket on Rhodes Avenue in Studio City, he looked at the houses and trees that framed the street. Terry had seen many changes when he came back from Seattle. He saw that "The Valley", the oft-used term for the San Fernando Valley, had grown to over a million people. Terry and his wife felt that this growth was mainly due to the charm of the custom homes with a "reasonable commute" (at least defined in LA terms) from Downtown Los Angeles to be less than an hour at rush hour traffic times. Terry loved the telephone repair job. It had a lot of freedom and was never boring.

The trouble address was in a part of Studio City that was north of Ventura Boulevard, a few blocks east of Jerry's Deli. The homes were older, but had been renovated, and were the farthest thing from track-home estates. They had character and uniqueness that had helped buoy property values, even in the last few years. However, the telephone plant had not been renovated. There were still aerial poles running along the back yards of these homes.

Terry hadn't climbed a pole in months, but today even that

seemed like a treat. He knocked on the front door, but got no answer. He went next door to ask for backyard access and was greeted by as foul a man as you could ever meet.

No one liked Marvin Schultz, the neighbor. Marvin worked very hard at this. He never spoke to neighbors except to yell and complain. He never tipped at restaurants and always went to the same ones. He was routinely rude—and good at it.

"Why should I let you in my yard?" he barked with his face nearly pressing on the security screen.

"Your neighbors would do the same for you if your phone wasn't working," offered Terry, as he covered his smile by touching his mustache.

"I don't care what they would do. You can go, but you are responsible for any damage," Marvin yelled as he slammed the door.

So, when the big explosion happened and the telephone hard hat hit his back door, Marvin was fully charged to rip into this telephone guy. He picked up the hard hat, which he saw had made a dent in his back door. They would pay for this. He stomped around the detached garage and started yelling as he looked up. The sun was directly in Marvin's eyes, so he positioned himself where the telephone pole blocked the sun. He enjoyed looking into the faces of people when he was yelling at them. Marvin couldn't see the telephone guy's face—or head, for that matter. He stepped to the left to get a better angle and kicked what he thought was a ball, thinking, "Those damn kids in back won't get this ball back." Marvin yelled the entire time he circled the telephone pole.

Then Marvin looked down and promptly threw up. For once, he was no longer yelling. Marvin wasn't even talking—and with his head disconnected from his body, neither was Terry.

As Terry opened the cable sheath, his nose had itched. His brain had sent a signal to his arm to scratch. That thought and his telephone service would not be "bridged." His headless body still hung on from the pole by his safety belt.

WHAT'S IN A NAME?

"Why?"

There were still days where he couldn't understand what his mom was thinking. Days like today when a not-so-good lawyer decided to "out" him in a ridiculous effort to impugn his credibility. He was there to testify about telephone records—calls made and received by a thoroughbred scumbag dope dealer. His job included various court appearances.

"What is your full name, Mr. Connecticut?"

"Objection!" said the prosecutor.

"Overruled!" the judge quickly responded.

"Bo Connecticut," he responded.

"No, your full legal name, please."

"Bozo Connecticut, no middle name."

The laughter in the courtroom came every time.

"You're the Bozo responsible for finding and identifying these records."

"We have all had our fun, Mr. Shapiro," the judge said, "Please ask questions that have some relevance."

"No more questions, your honor." The prosecutor smoothed his too-wide tie and returned to his seat.

☦

Sure, no one ever gave any credence to it, but the response to his name had gotten old, if only to him. In grade school, high school, and with every new person he met, there was this giddy juvenile settling-in period that he had to endure. It was never funny to him.

His mother did really have a sense of humor, but it was not apparent when she and an equally alcoholic admin nurse filled out the birth certificate forty-two years ago while finishing a half-gallon of one of her two most favorite wines—"red." While watching a local TV afternoon show in the private room at the hospital, featuring the famous (at least, at the time, famous) red-haired Bozo the clown. The nurse, matching glass for glass with his mother, thought the clown was cute. Enough wine had been consumed by his recovering mother and supportive nurse that they decided they thought the clown's name was also cute. It could have been worse: they might have been watching *Lassie*.

His name. Bozo. It had provided him with a higher level of excitement than the name of "Fred" would have, but all things considered, he could have lived with "Jim."

He really didn't resent his mom too much. Certainly, it was not the same story as the Johnny Cash song about "A Boy Named Sue"—Bozo never liked that song, never liked Johnny Cash, and never liked country music. Some of it was related to the name. Bozo.

Probably the main reason he didn't resent his mother was because she would always take his side of any issue. There really was nothing like a mother for unconditional love. He remembered the time in third grade Sister Jean Robert had called his mom from work, and she couldn't get there until almost four o'clock. Only he and Sister Jean Robert were there from when school was dismissed until his mother's arrival—or perhaps better described, her entrance. She arrived with the pastor, Monsignor James O'Flaherty, on her arm. Both had a nice buzz from an afternoon of drinking at the Fireside Inn. The liquid-enhanced joy was clear to Bozo, but it was not clear to the nun. It was also clear to Bozo and probably half the parish that old Jim O'Flaherty was quite smitten with Mrs. Connecticut. The nun also missed this nuance.

There is a pecking order in the Catholic church. At least, Bo thought there had been one when he was a child. All bishops were afraid of the Pope (except the Jesuits, who felt both spiritually and intellectually superior to the Pontiff); all priests were afraid of bishops (except Jim O'Flaherty, who had a special relationship with the Cardinal; no one really knew why); all nuns were afraid of the priests (no exceptions); and all regular parishioners were afraid of the nuns.

Nuns were always telling you how you would burn in hell for eternity. He remembered how, in the fifth grade, Sister Mary Anthony told the class that the urges the children were feeling needed to be ignored. People mature at different rates, so Christopher Burns assumed that "the urge" meant "going to the bathroom."

He routinely wet his pants three times a week.

Then when Sister Mary Anthony asked the children if they were willing to burn in hell for a few brief seconds of pleasure, she was stunned when Dickie Anderson blurted out, "Sister, you must be doing it wrong. You can get it to feel good for almost five minutes if you do it right." Dickie started public school the following Monday.

All these thoughts were running through Bo's mind as he was held in the principal's office after an altercation at school. Glenn Llewellyn had been making fun of his name again, but added insult to his mother—"the stupid slut"—and Bo had responded in kind. Public school, which had been described by the good sisters as a den of iniquity (a term few understood, but in a tone that all understood), was beginning to look like Bo's next destination. He sat with his fear until he saw his mom walk in the door with her "pecking order" on her arm.

"So sorry I'm late. Jim and I lost track of the time," she said. Sister Jean Robert said nothing, but her jaw dropped, obviously scandalized by the first name reference to the priest. The opposite effect showed on Father O'Flaherty's face as he beamed from the combined impact of his
mother's charm and a significant amount of Jack Daniels.

"Gotta be gettin' along myself," said Monsignor O'Flaherty. "Take good care of Mrs. Connecticut, will ya, Sister?"

The monsignor was born in Ireland 60 years ago and "decided" to be a priest 55 years ago when his mother told him he is going to be a priest. Irish mothers often spelled out details of their son's lives (and the monsignor's mother was clearly one of this group).

She had assigned his older brother to be a doctor and his younger brother to be a lawyer. Her health, spiritual and legal needs were taken care of. The monsignor also was a benevolent despot of a pastor, so, in his mind (and the nun's), Mrs. Connecticut would indeed be taken care of.

The nun's jaw sank a little lower as she slowly nodded. "Well, Mrs. Connecticut, Bozo has gotten himself into serious trouble fighting with the Llewellyn boy and…"

"Excuse me, Sister," my mother interrupted, then turned to Bozo. "Is this true?"

"Yeah, Mom, he said you were a slut, so I popped him in the nose, and he went crying to Sister." It was one of the better performances in his young life to highlight the insult to his mom, and he suspected it would get more sympathy than, "Yeah, the jerk made fun of my name."

The use of the word "slut" had an interesting effect on the sister's already sagging jaw. Bozo was beginning to think it was becoming unhinged, like a snake's. It had an even more interesting effect on his mom. She leaned over with her face about an inch away from the nun's, asking, "Where is the Llewellyn twerp?" Her whisper made both Bozo and the nun shiver.

"Mrs. Llewellyn took him to the hospital," the nun whispered, although her whisper sounded scared. Her jaw seemed to be raised because she was swallowing a lot. Maybe it was the smell of Jack Daniels.

"Why the fuck is my son being held here?"

The nun's jaw dropped again. So did Bozo's.

Then, as if nothing had been said at all, his mother smiled and said, "Bo, darling, get your things and let's go."

It became apparent that Bozo's mom was not a regular parishioner, because she definitely was not afraid of nuns—and, after that, neither was Bozo.

The next day, which Bozo thought would be his last at Our Lady of Grace, Glenn Llewellyn stood in front of the class apologizing to Mrs. Connecticut, Bozo, all women, the Blessed Virgin Mary and Our Lady of Grace. A side benefit was that Bozo got all the help he needed from the nuns with his schoolwork, and the benefit of the doubt on any altercation (although there weren't many). The nuns were terrified of a parent/teacher conference. The other benefit was that Bozo didn't think he was going to burn in hell for a few brief seconds of pleasure. He never did ask Dickie Anderson how to make it last five minutes. Still, Bozo would have liked his mom better if he would have been named "Jim." The only saving grace was that he could go by Bo, a name now popularized by Bo Jackson, who was a superstar at both baseball and football. His fame had been enhanced by an advertising campaign that cited things like "Bo knows football, Bo knows baseball or Bo knows cereal while holding a box of Wheaties."

However, among the many things that Bo Jackson knows, the one that he is probably the happiest about is that Bo knows his name isn't Bozo.

☦

He was sitting at Starbucks, watching the baristas hustle through orders and reflecting on his name, when his self-pitying thoughts were interrupted.

"Hey Bo!"

Bill Martini slid into the seat next to Bo, pointed to his glass, and held up two fingers to the barista. Bill had called Bo earlier and asked him to meet him at Starbucks.

"Hello, William."

"Oh, formal today. Must have gotten your feelings hurt in court."

"It's so childish, and I get tired of it."

Bill countered, "It's funny every time. None of the judges stop it. It never influences the jury. They can see you're a clown even without the name."

Bo laughed. Bill had been a friend—his best friend—since high school. They both had joined the army right after graduation, signing up in the buddy system. They were instantly shipped to different places—"needs of the service"—Bill to a motor pool and Bo to the MPs. Their deployments eventually re-connected in Iraq. They each served for four years, then started working for the telephone company the same week, entering in the same orientation class. Again, they went different ways. Bill became a driver for company executives and Bo ultimately (after a few years as an Installer and then Installation Supervisor) became a Special Agent for the Chief Special Agents, the security group within the telephone company.

Bill wanted to talk to Bo about something personal, but changed his mind and instead brought up a job-related issue. "Can we talk shop a little bit? As you know, I often work out of hours, in the evening when executives attend dinners and events." Bill continued, "Our initial training had spoken to the fact that we were often in a personal or privileged position to see and hear things that should be kept confidential…"

Bo noticed that his friend seemed worried about something, and Bill was never like that.

Then, as a joke, Bo said, "Like priests, right?"

"Yeah," Bill responded. Bo was stunned that his joke didn't even get a smile.

"What's really going on, Bill?"

Bill looked around the table to see if anyone else was or could be listening. "I drive for the VP of Marketing and the President, mostly. The President is a class-A megalomaniac, but the VP of Marketing is a pretty good guy. However, I've been taking him to Lakers games and he often takes one of the technicians from the 'Bright Lights' program. You know, the folks from gang areas who were given the opportunity to take better jobs than just working at a fast-food place."

"Yes, our admin clerk is from that program," Bo replied.

"Well, they have been bringing girls, too—some of them work for us—and I get the distinct feeling that certainly booze is part of the routine, but also some drugs."

"Wait Bill, you're not a prude… or a priest, for that matter. What's bothering you?"

"The VP, Tim Wallace, is married and the technician, DeMarius Thomas, seems to be steering the ship. He is determining where and when we go anywhere. You would be surprised how I become invisible as they say and do things in front of me that are beyond inappropriate. The bottom line is that I think that Tim has a problem with drugs that has not been an issue at all for the previous three years."

"So, what do you want to do?" Bo challenged his friend.

Just then, both their cells went off.

BLOOD BROTHERS

Freddie Kanes sat in his house in one of the nicest areas in South Central. He didn't want any criminal activity in the area that might bring police to his house. He had been the co-leader of one of the sects of the Hoover Criminals (a descendant from the Crips) for some time. He and DeMarius ran the group together, and it was unique to have co-leadership. It was also unique that both were college graduates. The house remained in Freddie's grandmother's name even though she had passed ten years ago. The outside of the house was well kept up—paint fresh, lawn mowed—but remained unremarkable. He wanted no attention at all brought to his home—at least on the outside.

Inside the house was another story, except for an office just at the entry. The office was a converted bedroom with an attached bathroom. The remodeled room appeared as plain and practical as the outside. The furniture was purposely distressed. The couch had cushions of many colors and one had been purposely stained with coffee. The desktop had been similarly abused. All had been done so that Freddie appeared not to be greedy or extravagant.

If someone looked closely, however, they might notice the house was outfitted for a person in a less than savory line of work. The windows were bulletproof. The bathroom was a safe room, as the walls and ceiling were steel under the plaster. The sliding steel door inside the bathroom was specifically designed to be hidden. It also was spring-loaded and could snap shut, completely cutting anything (wood, concrete block, etc.) in its path. It had once sliced a chair in half as Freddie inadvertently hit the close switch as he was sliding a chair inside. False panels hid electronic gear controlling hidden cameras and microphones both inside and outside the house.

The work had been done by an independent contractor from Nebraska. The contractor had no family, had been paid well—and in cash—during the four months of work, and was put up by Freddie in a hotel near the house during the job. He had shot himself eating a shotgun the week he returned to his home—an "unfortunate suicide." No one knew about these modifications except for Freddie. Well, no one alive.

The rest of the house behind the front rooms was richly decorated. It had hardwood floors, lovely handmade Indian rugs, a superb entertainment system and a chef's dream of a kitchen. Most of the furniture was from Ethan Allen and none of it was distressed. But very few people saw the rest of the house.

For a gang member, Freddie was unusual. He appeared like anyone else on the street. He saw no need to brandish his gang membership or his money. Often, gang members wore several gold chains that would easily have rivaled Mr. T's. Freddie saw this as an invitation for the law to stop him or rival gangs to hassle him. He did have one tattoo on his left abdomen that no one ever saw—"DeMarius and Freddie Together" surrounded by two hawks with banners draped from each claw, reading "Birds of a feather."

†

Freddie scratched his full beard as he thought about DeMarius. He had grown the beard as soon as facial hair started to cover the acne damage on his face. It had softened his face considerably, but he had earned a reputation by then that commanded respect and fear.

DeMarius had no beard. Freddie thought that there was no reason for DeMarius to cover his beautiful face. Freddie reflected on their long friendship, how they met and their early gang involvement.

Freddie was tall for his age, and even as a teen, looked old enough to drive. He was used often as a driver because he did not attract much attention from others. He also could convince others to do his work for him and had developed a close-knit following, even as a twelve-year old. He often protected others in his clique from the OG (original gang members). They tolerated his requests because Freddie had become a particularly reliable runner. This had also created significant personal loyalties to Freddie. Freddie saw that most gang leaders were cautious of anyone with "leadership skills." They even saw that gathering of Freddie's band as humorous and causing no actual harm. The leaders who were not arrested or killed in drive-by's over the next five years were the first victims of Freeway Freddie's subtle assassinations.

Freddie never felt sorry for DeMarius—thought his state of life was cool. DeMarius had been a bit of a celebrity at age six. He was found caring for his mother's body (an overdose) after calling 911—a call that made all the networks. It was a small voice saying, "My mother is not moving. I am staying with her, but I am scared. Please help me." The call led to an outpour of donations, scholarships, and a bit of celebrity.

The real story was that indeed his mom was a drug addict. She was in a crack haze and wanted more. She had planned her continued high and left a needle with an extra dose. DeMarius didn't even hate her for the years of neglect. He was just tired of it. He saw that there was more stuff and, since he had prepared it for her many times, just filled the syringe completely.

"Can I do it, Mommy?"

"Yeah, baby."

DeMarius depressed the syringe and held it while his mother convulsed for about a minute and then became still. He waited because he wanted to make sure she was dead, and he didn't want her to wake up. After about 20 minutes, he went to the phone and made the 911 call.

The emergency folks and the police felt great sorrow for the wide-eyed little boy. They assumed he was not crying from shock, rather than not caring about his mother at all. He was an angelic-looking, beautiful boy—an attribute that would serve him well in the future. A policeman who had a press connection made a call about the incident. The reporter got the 911 call and the story exploded. Trusts were set up for the donated money and the scholarship. The grandmother took custody and, besides a bit of a drinking problem, provided DeMarius with a good home. She didn't take any of his money—not when she paid the property taxes on the home she fully owned.

Freddie met DeMarius when some teenager was kicking DeMarius in an alley. Neither DeMarius nor Freddie ever knew the reason for the teenager's attack. Freddie did not really care about the kicking of the boy. It meant nothing to him. He just didn't like the look of the teenager. It was dusk, but there was no one around. Freddie came up and asked if he could help kick the crap out of DeMarius.

"Sure, little man."

Freddie kicked DeMarius's legs as hard as he could. The teenager, probably 15, laughed so hard his head leaned back. Freddie quickly pulled his knife and cut into his inside left thigh. The blood exploded out. The teenager fell and grabbed his wound, opened his mouth, but never said a word. It may have been the surprise; it may have been shock.

"Get up, let's go," Freddie calmly said to DeMarius. DeMarius hopped up and they ran down the alley and went to DeMarius's house. DeMarius's grandmother made dinner for both the boys, glad her grandson finally had made a friend. She thought that the trauma of his mom's death was the reason he had no friends, but DeMarius was happy to be a loner.

Freddie did not know why he had intervened to save DeMarius. He had seen a character in a movie cut someone's inner thigh, and their key artery bled out. He wondered if it was true. He knew intuitively that it was dangerous in South Central Los Angeles without some sort of group of friends or a friend you could trust, but there was no concern or righteousness in his motives. Later, while at school, they looked up "sociopath" and felt that the description had application to each of them. They also felt that "psychopath" had an application. Almost no one knew their true feelings—or lack of them—as they were both experts at mimicking any and all emotions. Both boys realized that some friendship was necessary in the neighborhood. They also realized that they saw and "felt"—or, more correctly, "didn't feel"—the same way about other people. The necessary friendship and lack of feelings had created a bond between them.

This trait allowed each of them to be whatever they wanted to be or, more precisely, whatever "you" wanted them to be. It served DeMarius well with the emergency folks, the police, the teachers at school and his grandmother and now with Freddie.

The alley incident slowly got out and the younger "toughs" gave both boys—now inseparable—a wide berth. The older gang members thought they were a great asset and used them appropriately. Those older members foolishly assumed they were mentors and idols of the younger two.

They were together so much their moniker had been FreMar, which, of course, was like Bennifer (Ben Affleck and Jennifer Lopez) or TomKat (Tom Cruise and Katie Holmes) contractions of their names. Neither DeMarius nor Freddie necessarily liked the name, but they didn't like the ones that praised violence more. It also reinforced the thinking that they had each other's backs.

Unlike other gang members, both Freddie and DeMarius had "disappeared" for three and a half years while getting their college degrees. Both their grandmothers had secured promises from their grandsons about this. There was remarkably little reaction from the gang when they left, as many saw it as their chance to "move up" in the organization. Freddie and DeMarius left the neighborhood with enough money to pay for rent in Alhambra, plus both tuition bills at Junior College and Cal State LA. They both excelled in their studies. DeMarius in the arts; Freddie in the sciences.

Recently, they had expanded their efforts for growing the drug business and had used DeMarius's celebrity to place gang members in a jobs program that offered more than a McDonald's-type job. Freddie's crew had over thirty gang members in jobs with the telephone company. A long-time City Councilman had remembered the stories about young DeMarius and had reached out to both the telephone company and the two boys about their interest. DeMarius's "celebrity" from the past would make him a poster boy for the program, plus their college educations made them attractive candidates. Freddie was first to see the potential of the program for the gang and himself and DeMarius always enjoyed the spotlight. Thus, the pilot of the 'Bright Lights' program began.

DeMarius had a repair tech job. The idea was to use these positions to gain technical skills and to learn information from internal reports. They routinely monitored other gang's phone calls and used this information to steal incoming drugs. Information gathering and its sharing and use was limited to only Freddie and DeMarius. When others were included in a plot so they could complete a heist, they were quickly killed.

OCCASIONAL CRIME SCENE

Originally, the title of Bozo's job was "Special Agent," but it had been changed to "Investigator" some years ago. No one liked the change because the title of "Special Agent" had had some "coolness", as it mimicked an FBI title. Like many changes over the years, it seemed that lawyers had a hand in it, but no one knew for sure. Bozo's duties involved liaising with the courts or police, investigating impropriety of employees with the company's equipment or money, and occasionally investigating potential issues of workplace conduct.

Bo was responsible for all of Southern California, from the Mexican border to the Ventura County line at Santa Barbara to the east state line of California. At the time, telephone companies had geographic monopolies. Santa Barbara and Santa Monica were General Telephone's territory, so it was only a rare occasion where any security issue crossed these boundaries, at least for security agents dealing with any. Deaths of any kind were rare, but murders were almost non-existent. Almost always, they became the complete jurisdiction of the local police. He remembered that this was one of the few times he actually went to a crime scene. He had been to a few in the army while in Iraq. It was never a pleasant experience. He had received two calls—one from the normal channels, where the police had asked to have someone from the telephone company connect with them ASAP on a recent crime. The detective in the office gave Bozo the address of the crime scene and told him to report to Detective Healy.

The second call had come from his boss, Carol Dellamor. Carol was young for a director-level job. At one time, Directors were typically 50-year-old-plus white men with the beginning of a pot belly and thinning hair. Pacific Telephone had agreed to a consent decree wherein hiring and promotion opportunities would go more often to women and minorities. Carol was attractive, whip-smart and 34 years old. Many were jealous of her, but the diversity of the hiring program was a real commitment of Pacific Bell and she was an example of a successful outcome. She knew what she didn't know and was a quick learner and an expert delegator. Most on the team had overcome their initial concerns and liked her. She had replaced William (not "Bill") Morris, who did almost nothing and had acquired the behind-his-back nickname of "Wild Bill."

Bill had thirty-five years when he retired. He'd said at his thirty-year service anniversary party, "I've given thirty of the best years of my life to this company; now, I'm going to give it five of the worst!"

When Carol asked what the investigation team had going in her first week, it seemed like micro-management compared to William

Turner's hands-off management style. Also, she did a good job at shielding her team from the bureaucracy and politics.

She told Bo that this was a serious situation. Someone was dead; she didn't know if it was one of theirs, or someone else. The story was a little vague, but the uppity ups wanted someone on site and wanted a report back ASAP. She said she received the call from the Installation manager, who was doing periodic quality checks.

Bo had driven straight there once he got the call, and that meant it took 45 minutes to go from downtown to the Valley on the 101 Freeway at rush hour. When he got there, he realized it was a neighborhood remarkably close to where Gloria and Jimmy (his wife and son) lived. The neighborhood had steadily become one of the nicer neighborhoods in Studio City as original owners had gotten older and sold to younger families, who had renovated the 40-year-old homes. The mature trees gave a serene feel that was significantly interrupted by police cars, fire trucks and an ambulance.

He asked the police woman at the yellow taped boundary for Detective Healy. Bo recognized him right away as a father of a boy on his son's soccer team.

When Healy came over to the police tape, Bo introduced himself as the requested representative from the telephone company. Healy was a big man. His brown skin was flawless, so much so, he could have been a model for skin care products. Bo was constantly reminded about Gloria's concern for skin health and care, so he noticed people's skin.

"Hi, you're Jimmy's dad, right?" Healy said as he waved Bo past the tape and the protecting officer. "I'm John, Brian's dad. I didn't realize you worked for the telephone company."

"Yeah, I didn't realize you were a police officer. I'm Bo," he said as they shook hands.

"Bo, I don't tell people I am a police officer that very much. It gets varied responses, 80 percent of which I would like to avoid. What do you do at the telephone company?" Healy was thinking "public relations."

"I am in the Security group in our Investigations department. I received two calls to come out to check out the scene. One was an internal company call from a supervisor through my boss. The other was from LAPD to check in with you."

Healy smiled a bit. Bo didn't quite recognize it as "mall cop cynicism"—the rent-a-cop evaluation of any corporate security—but he caught an air of superiority coming from the detective. He followed Healy, whose height blocked the setting sun as they walked around the house. Healy provided some nice shade for Bo, who stood at 5'11".

As Bo walked in the shadow of Healy, he noticed a paunch around the detective's beltline. Bo enjoyed that he was still thin—as much from genetics as from any exercise program.

Healy half turned and asked, "Do you know what we have here?"

"No, except that someone is dead."

"They didn't tell you who it was? That's why I wanted someone here. We think it was one of your technicians. We have his wallet and company ID, but he is not recognizable because of the explosion. That supervisor who called you is here, but she is so distressed that she hasn't been able to talk with us."

Bo stopped walking suddenly. He tilted his head and asked

Healy, "What explosion? Hey, I was just sent to be here with no briefing at all. What do you mean, 'explosion?' None of our techs carry anything even potentially explosive. This might happen in the army, but not with the telephone company."

Healy stopped, turned, and fully faced Bo. He considered Bo's response and thought that maybe his PR or rent-a-cop evaluation might not be what Bo is. "Okay, I'm sorry. Do you have any background in this type of work?"

Recognizing a change in tone, Bo said, "I have been doing this for eight years with the telephone company. Not many deaths. And even when there were, they were not our people—traffic accidents, stuff like that. Prior to that, I was an MP for six years—two tours in Iraq. Some of it was in Kuwait. I saw plenty of deaths there. It doesn't make me a police officer, but I am not a mall cop, either. But we haven't had anything like this at the phone company."

Healy shook his head. "Sorry again. First, I thought you were a PR guy, then a rent-a-cop type. I don't think the technician caused the explosion. I think this may have been an ambush for whomever got up that pole and worked on the lines. But, for sure, someone is going to consider this as some sort of terrorism." Healy continued, "We can't recognize the deceased because his face is gone completely, but his head is somewhat intact—just not connected anymore. Our people are searching the yard, the roof of the garage, and the driveway for pieces."

Bo asked "Sorry, head not connected?"

Healy sighed, "The body was still hanging on the pole. The ID says his name was Terry Simpson. I was hoping you could help me find out if he was here on his own or on the job. His company truck is parked out front, so we think he was doing his job. The fact that this is an explosion gets everybody's terrorism threshold up a notch or two."

"I can find that out quickly." Bo grabbed his notebook from his back pocket and began making notes. "Any collateral damage? People love to sue the telephone company, and I'll get asked that before they even ask his name."

Healy looked down the driveway at all the techs and police officers on the scene. "No, this was a tight directional blast. I think the blast centered on his nose, but we don't know how the bomb was attached. His hat blew off and dented the neighbor's door. You will not want to talk with him unless you have the need to want to hit someone."

Healy continued, "We just need to know if he was here because of work."

Bo said, "I can help there as well, because we keep records of this type of stuff—almost 95 percent accurate. But if you will walk with me a half a block, I can probably show you. If we are anything, we are very uniform. I am positive whatever was on this pole is on the pole four houses down. If I see it, I can describe it and get you details later."

Healy grabbed one of the crime scene techs and the three walked down the street. After securing access to enter the yard of the house 4 lots north from a pretty blonde teenager, which Healy noticed was much easier with the police badge and a friendlier neighbor, Bo climbed the pole. He had gotten his hard hat, climbing belt (fully stocked with appropriate tools) and climbing gaffs. He didn't need to use the climbing gaffs as he used the ladder the crime tech had brought so he could easily reach the pole steps, which were 10 feet off the ground for safety reasons—not facilitating a climb from wandering teenagers or curious 10-year-old's.

"I wouldn't open whatever is up there. We don't know if this is an isolated instance," Healy's crime scene guy yelled up to Bo.

"Don't worry, I am not touching anything. How big would the explosive be?" Bo could see the terminal had not been touched for a long time.

"About the size of a slab of butter." The tech thought that it would be formed to be directional as it exploded, and it would be pointed in shape.

Bo was curious. "Would it need to be protected from the elements?"

The tech considered this. "I don't know, but I think so. If it were left out in the open, it would have been apparent that it was a dangerous thing, and most people would not have touched it."

"No offense, Bo, but if Simpson was planting it, we could have another scenario," Healy offered, "Was he an unhappy employee? Wanted to get more overtime? Had a grudge against one of these neighbors?"

"I get it, you are considering all options," Bo said as he climbed down. "But most likely, the explosive was inside what we call a ready access terminal. This is an older type of outside plant. It was being replaced with an underground outside fiber plant. It just wasn't here yet. Also, anyone could have opened this up. It did not take a technical person's skills to open the terminal—no special tools or anything. As far as our technician doing this, I wouldn't understand any terrorist motive—killing the next tech or some random fool who would climb the pole? There is plenty of overtime available. But I'll find out if he was dispatched here and what kind of guy he was. You should have all of this by mid-morning tomorrow. Just a thought, it may be worthwhile looking at the pole back there and its surroundings for any signs of recent climbing before the tech got there."

The tech smiled. "That's a good idea."

"I'd like it to be faster than tomorrow morning. Can you update me as you get more info? Here's my number," Healy said, offering his card. "I appreciate the input and look forward to working with you. You know, I have never said that to anybody before," Healy laughed.

Bo asked, "Anything else?"

Healy remembered that when he arrived that morning, Mrs. Anderson had met him at the street and graciously offered her house for "that poor girl." Healy didn't know that it would take almost a half-hour to get the girl into the house and settled down. It was not because Jenny Lee was upset, and she clearly was, but the real price was listening to the life history of Mrs. Anderson from her move to California from Illinois up to her daughter getting the job in the forestry service. He had introduced himself as Lieutenant several times, but she kept calling him Sergeant.

"Well, immediately?" Healy's smile vanished. "You could help us with Jenny Lee, Terry's supervisor, who is a real basket case. Evidently, she saw the headless body on the pole. She is inside the neighbor's house here with a very nice lady, Mrs. Anderson. Come on, I will introduce you."

"I actually know her." Bo replied. They had met before when

Bo was following up on an "incident" happening at the garage. As they were walking back to the crime scene, Bo saw the ambulance leaving. Neither Healy nor Bo had mentioned seeing the body and/or head.

"John, can I make a call to my boss to let her know I am here and give her some details?" Bo asked.

"Sure," said Healy, "But leave the decapitation and next of kin obligation to the police for now."

Bo, with wide eyes, responded, "Not a problem!"

JENNY LEE

Bo and John Healy walked up to a storybook of a house, tan with white trim, a white ranch fence, and a big white swing on the front porch. Mrs. Anderson opened the door before the men reached the porch and said, "Sergeant. Healy, she has stopped crying. She is in my daughter's bedroom. She really is quite a lovely girl."

Healy introduced Bo as a telephone company security man, and predictably Mrs. Anderson called him "Sergeant Connecticut." As they entered the bedroom, Bo was almost breathless. When they had met before, she was quite beautiful, but was self-assured, confident and emotionless. Now, Jenny Lee was on the bed with her makeup streaking down her face, her hair matted from the combination of mud and tears, her hands filthy, with her already too short skirt hiked up an extra inch, and, still, the most striking woman Bo had ever seen. Her figure was hidden by her fetal position, but her electric green eyes shined on her smooth-skinned face. As he thought this, Bo blinked, realizing his new-found skin evaluating addiction.

"Sergeant Connecticut will take care of Miss Lee, Mrs. Anderson," said Lt. Healy, giving up on explaining ranks or roles.

Bo looked at Jenny and immediately did the inevitable comparison with Gloria that he often did. She was shorter than Gloria, but she smiled with her eyes at him.

Gloria, even when he was living at the house, had not smiled with her eyes at Bo for the longest time. He thought that maybe this "comparing" was a character defect, but he could remember that he didn't do it when he was happy with Gloria and she was happy with him. He clearly was doing it now. Bo wondered if others looked at people and pictured them with the requisite 2.3 children and the white picket fence around the two-story colonial house, then compared them with the most "real" view of their own relationship. Since Gloria was not happy with him now, his "real" view of his relationship was much different.

Bo's relationship was currently offering him separation from a wife who hated his work, who gave him every other weekend and random weeknights with his son, and who allowed him to live in an above-garage apartment five blocks away. He convinced himself that he was not disloyal or shallow to entertain a fantasy with this lovely lady.

"Why don't we get out of here? You could use the fresh air, and I could use something to eat." Bo saw her wince at the mention of food. He gave her his arm, but he finally had to put an arm around her because her legs were so unsteady. Jenny stopped and went to Mrs. Anderson and they embraced for almost a minute. Jenny stopped and said, "Thank you for your graciousness."

"No problem, sweetie, it was like having my daughter home again." She then looked at Bo. "Take good care of this girl, Sergeant Connecticut."

They drove in silence for about two miles along Ventura Boulevard, past a number of restaurants that made his stomach growl. He finally asked her if she wanted to go home, and she seemed to awaken from a stupor to look at him.

"No... no... can we just drive for a while?"

"No problem," he lied. He was starving, but he didn't mind just being with such a beautiful lady. She even looked nice with the vomit crusted on her collar.

He knew that she couldn't have been charmed by his car, a black '87 Taurus that he bought as a used rental from one of the Woodland Hills car agencies. He had come to hate the car. It was a 4-cylinder model, and it was truly gutless. Gloria thought that it was a great car for Bo since she thought he drove too fast. Bo thought it was just another example of her need for control. Another reason he hated the car. At least it was running this week. He had spent over $1500 in repair costs, and the most frustrating thing was that the costs were not covered by the warranty. Every time he saw a "quality" ad by Ford, he would vow to write the president of the company, but he never did.

After driving for about 20 minutes in silence, "I'd like to stop, and you said you were hungry. Could we stop somewhere?" Jenny asked.

"There is a place up here that has pretty good eggs, quiche, and salad," said Bo, thinking of something mild for her stomach.

Jenny said, "Fine."

While driving there, Jenny gave the background on Terry Simpson. "He was a great guy. Been a tech for a long time. Left and then came back about—exactly 5 years ago. His service got bridged today—and...." She sobbed a little. "Of all days. He was as happy as you might imagine. They had a trip to Hawaii planned." She went on to tell him that she had checked the trouble ticket and had been assigned it. She said that the customer requested a certain technician, but he couldn't take it.

Bo pulled the Taurus into the driveway next to VExpress and took a ticket from the valet parking attendant. They got a window seat, which was pretty hard when you arrived after 10:00pm. VExpress underwent a metamorphosis from breakfast house to coffee house to "meat market" (where all the young and restless tried to get "rested") and finally to a late diner place. Bo and Jenny were in late dinner mode.

While Jenny freshened up, Bo left a voicemail for Healy with the details from Jenny. He told Healy he would go to the garage in the morning to see if there were any other items of interest.

Bo felt as uncomfortable as he would on a date, but Jenny seemed to be distracted, as her attention became focused only after repeating any question at least twice. Bo asked no more questions.

"It is hard to see anyone dead. I saw way too many in Iraq—and its impact is not diminished by seeing even one more. It is especially hard to see someone you know. It is alright to be upset," said Bo. It seemed like she was disappointed in herself for being upset.

This seemed to almost break a dam of feelings from Jenny.

While she was quietly crying, Bo was remembering when they met.

Normally, the folks in the garage would have been protective and secretive of someone from the investigator's office, but they knew Bo. He had been there before.

Five years ago, an anonymous letter had been forwarded to the security office that a manager had actually beaten one of the technicians at the garage. They were complaining about an unsafe work environment. This occurred during a time where people were encouraged to use the company ombudsman program to bring illegal, unfair, or unsafe issues to light that people felt either would not necessarily be given a proper investigation by the local management or they were afraid of repercussions for bringing the issue forward. About 20 percent of these complaints pointed out some real problems—ironically, not always the reported problem—and 20 percent were some unfounded complaints from employees using the system to bother a targeted person, and the rest fell somewhere in between. There were about fifty complaints every year now—the first year of the program, there had been two-hundred and fifty complaints, and the vast majority, as William Turner so delicately put it, were "crap."

However, one case from the first year of the ombudsman program was assigned to Bo and involved Jenny. The atmosphere was different during that first visit. Nobody liked the security office or the people in it. Bo believed it was a similar attitude that the police department's internal affairs group received from the rank and file.

Fifty-plus years ago, the technicians were called installers and repairmen. And they were all men. This was a man's job. The district manager had second-level managers, who were regarded as kings by subordinates and management and had absolute power over almost everything except firing. The district manager had power firing. Bo had seen in Iraq that "absolute power corrupts absolutely." It was true today as it was then.

"Wild Bill" Morris had entertained his team with story after story where there was close to sadism occurring with certain employees. Some of the managers would take a tech behind the garage and Morris would instruct the tech to "beat the crap out of him. If the cruelty was excessive—that is, an employee received more than one beating—then a second-level or a district manager was encouraged to retire. It was not public knowledge, but everyone at the company knew about it.

People didn't remember this time or weren't around anymore. So when the report came in, William Turner had come to Bo's desk, which he had done exactly three times in all Bo's days at the company. Once he was so drunk from lunch, he asked Bo to drive him home. Another time when he was leaving the office on his final day. He'd said, "Thanks for the ride." And then this time, when he said, "I want you to report directly to me on all aspects of this case."

Bo spoke with a second-level manager, saying, "I don't know of anything like this, but I know that none of my managers would do anything like this." It became a mantra, almost verbatim, from not only the managers, but all the techs in the garage. There were a couple of new female techs that hesitated with their answers, and Bo concluded that they didn't know anything, but were afraid that this was a place that would allow it. Still, no one varied from the script—except Jenny.

"Do you know of any incident like this?" Bo had asked her.

She said, "Yes." Bo waited about a minute and didn't say anything. Neither did Jenny. Silence is usually a great interview tool, but Bo felt that if he had sat there quietly for a year, Jenny would have also.

"Do you know who the people are?"

"Yes," Jenny quickly replied

He gave up the silence quickly.

"What are their names?"

"I won't tell you."

"Pardon me?" Bo was stunned.

"I won't tell you. It is none of my business."

Bo normally would have reacted by putting pressure on her, or tried to reassure her that she would be protected from reprisal. But she had said it in such a fashion that he actually believed it was none of her business.

"Can you tell me what happened?"

"Sure, one of the managers had taken a completely rude and obnoxious technician out behind the garage to counsel him. The employee grabbed the manager, said several unacceptable things. Then, the manager counseled the employee verbally, emotionally, and physically."

"You've got to tell me."

"No, I don't."

"Why?"

"It was four months ago. The tech is now a model employee. If the details get out, he will get suspended or terminated. The manager will also get disciplined. I don't think that will do anybody any good."

"Still, other people here have got to feel threatened by this type of 'counseling.'"

Jenny countered, "Actually, I believe everyone knew about it. Just not the details."

"Someone was offended enough that they sent a letter to the ombudsman."

"They must be new."

Bo knew that as well. He thought as he was looking at Jenny that she almost transcended this conversation. She was so serene that she was clinical in her description and her logic. She was so beautiful that she was distracting. Her eyes and her skin were what models would sell their souls for. They were complemented by a hint of freckles that crossed the bridge of her petite nose. She was 5'8", slender, but with a strength that was present, but not displayed. And, best of all, she seemed almost indifferent about it.

She was not afraid of any reprisal. She just didn't think it was any of my business—or hers.

"Why are you telling me some but not all of it?"

"I was trying to be efficient, Mr. Connecticut."

"You know, I will probably find out what happened."

"Well, I told you what happened. And you may find out the 'who,' but you don't need to, and it wouldn't do any good; it would just cause more harm. But that is your decision, Mr. Connecticut."

The interview had been in her office at the garage. Jenny finished, stood, and began to walk out of her office. He started to say something, but he realized that the conversation was over as well. He had just interviewed a person who was much smarter than him in the cerebral sense, the practical sense, and the moral sense.

Like that day, Bo knew the truth was in the details. His mom used to say "the devil's in the details," but since she'd started going to AA, she modified the saying to "God is in the details."

☦

Jenny, unfortunately, had an affair with one of her crew, which by itself would not have caused any problems, but when she became pregnant and decided to keep the child as a single parent, the conservative nature of telephone people looked at her as clearly lacking upward mobility. Many of the employees had 20+ and 30+ years with the telephone company. They were ingrained with the values of another generation, which were more conservative. Many were at the higher levels of the company and their viewpoint was often mirrored by those who reported to them. By then, she was tied into the insurance and the security that she felt she needed for her son, who was now nine years old.

She had worked for the company for twelve years. She had told Bo once before, after several pitchers of margaritas, that her dad was embarrassed by her. His "moral standard" at Officer-level position couldn't tolerate something as scandalous as an unmarried mother. He refused to even see his grandson. This led to her parents' divorce. Her mom would not tolerate any separation from her grandson.

The divorce had a positive side effect. Her mother, Beverly, moved down and helped with her grandson. They lived less than a mile from the explosion, in a great neighborhood just east of Laurel Canyon and south of Ventura. And also, less than a mile from Bo's wife and son's place. Jenny and her mother had never commented on Bo's family's somewhat unique relationship. Bo had proven to be equally nonjudgmental, and that mutual acceptance had become the cement of their friendship. Jenny had stopped sobbing. She even opened up about herself a little bit.

Bo asked, "Does the father have any involvement with your son?"

Jenny said, "He quit the company. He left the state and I have no idea where he is. My son hasn't even asked about him. I've become suspicious of all men and if I did have a relationship with a man, I prefer to have an affair with a married man because it is safer. I know it would lead to nothing and it gives me an out."

She suddenly sat up quickly saying, "I can't believe I am talking about myself after what has happened to Terry. He was so nice and so happy this morning."

Bo looked out the window. "When I was in Iraq, we would hear of another company losing some people to IEDs placed around the cities. When it was someone in our crew or even one of our team, the conversation seemed to be about ourselves rather than the person killed. At first, that seemed self-centered and disrespectful. Someone even commented on it aloud once. The First Sergeant of our team said he had that experience in the past. He said, 'I even went to one of the Army's head doctors about it. He told us that life is precious, and we know it in our hearts and minds.' The doc hated the term 'survivor's guilt' because he thought it focused on ourselves. He felt that an intimate and violent loss just highlighted the waste of a life, and it was natural and not wrong for us to recognize the good things in our life or the things we want to have in our life. Then he said we should talk about every funny and good memory of the person we just lost."

Jenny then slowly smiled and told a story about Terry that was interrupted by her laughing so much, Bo never did understand it. She then talked about her father's abandonment, her mother's unconditional love, and her son's joy. Bo countered with his son's joy, his real love of his job, his mom and her drinking woes, and the separation status of his marriage.

Three hours later, they paid the bill.

OUR GANG

As Bo and Jenny were paying their bill in Sherman Oaks, about 20 miles southeast, another bill was coming due. Freddie Kane was fuming over a series of bad events that had begun to unravel his best effort to give some stability to his organization.

He had succeeded in his 27 years of life so far by enlisting and protecting an elite corps of lieutenants that insulated him from any effort by law enforcement to even arrest him. His nickname was either from rising so fast in drug trafficking or from his ability to fade into the hood after he was spotted.

Freddie was one of many gang members in South Central Los Angeles. Like many others, he began his gang career in grade school by watching out for police or other gangs and earning as much as $150.00 per day. His grandmother, who would clean other people's houses, would earn that in about a month.

In college, Freddie and DeMarius had also learned about the history of street gangs, gaining context that helped them become even stronger leaders when they returned to the streets.

Black street gangs had existed since the 1920s and had an original make-up of family members and close friends. There was limited criminal activity which had the purpose of promoting their "tough guy" image as well as providing a means of money.

From 1955 to 1965, there was a significant increase in the number and membership of gangs in South Central Los Angeles and Compton areas. Those gangs were more territorial groups than the traditional gangs of today. Usually, at parks, parties, or at high school sporting events, there were fights and some stabbings, but few shootings. It was almost modeled after the gangs romanticized in the musical West Side Story.

From 1965 to 1969, there was a tremendous decrease in gang activity due to the Vietnam war, the draft, and the progression of the Civil Rights movement. Potential gang members found themselves either in the military or involved in Black activism for civil rights.

It was in 1969 that the first Crips gang started in South Central Los Angeles. There are several stories where the name Crips comes from; some believe that it was derived from the comic book Tales from the Crypt. Others attribute it to an offshoot of a 1960s gang called the "Cribs."

Another story, told to Freddie by an original Crips gang member, says that Crips was due to some original members being handicapped, and the word cripple was abbreviated to "crip." Interestingly, the early Crips gangs carried walking sticks as a means of identification.

Probably the most believable story was that the gang members wanted a name indicating that they were the toughest and hardest thing imaginable. They thought about Superman—the only thing that could kill Superman was Kryptonite. Then, Kryptonite was spelled phonetically and shortened to "Crips."

The early Crips began terrorizing the local neighborhoods by theft, "protection", extortion and murder and then going to surrounding neighborhoods. These Crips developed a reputation early for being very violent and dangerous. Youths confronted with the Crips were forced to fight, flee, or give in to the barrage of robbery, extortion of money, or assault. Several neighborhoods formed gangs to protect themselves from Crips violence.

Other phenomena of the more recent gangs were the enlistment of the very young. In the older types of gangs, where there was mostly fighting, a gang member needed to be big and tough. They also started around the high schools, so this was the age group. There was no role for eight- to ten-year-old or even twelve- to fourteen-year-olds. Drugs provided new jobs for the younger group as well as a new market.

One gang which formed to protect itself from the Crips were a group of individuals from Piru Street in Compton. The "Compton Pirus" became the first Bloods gang in L.A. In the 1970s, the Pirus were very successful in confrontations with the Crips and became very powerful. Then, in the late 1970s, the Crips began to outnumber the Bloods, and the gang had increased steadily until present day, where Crips outnumber Bloods at a ratio of about three to one.

Newly formed gangs associated themselves with either Crips or Bloods. In the 1990's, the number of gangs in Los Angeles and

Compton were greater than any time before. A more sophisticated type of gang warfare developed and evolved in both weaponry and technique. The driveby shooting was introduced. There was a dramatic increase in assaults and homicides. It was generally as a result of younger members trying to impress their peers and the gang leaders. Crack cocaine had fueled the growth and the funding for all members.

Each gang had its own culture. The Crips adopted blue for their clothing to set them apart from other gang members. It is believed that the color was chosen from one of the school colors of Washington High School.

The Bloods chose the color red, one of Centennial High School's colors, and also because it was the color of blood.

Although the biggest division was between Crips and Bloods, there were almost three hundred gangs, or "sets." There were about 170 Crips gangs and approximately 70 Blood gangs, each formed on a geographical basis, like the Compton Crips or the Hoover Crips.

It was with the Hoover Crips that Freddie Kane started his gang career. He was promoted from his lookout role to "runner," where he transported supplies, weapons, or drugs. The gangs used the younger gang members because they were unlikely to receive anything more than probation for their first few offenses. Also, the younger members were used for the bloody retaliation.

When DeMarius and Freddie were in college, there was significant turnover in their gang in their absence. There were both alliances and feuds with other gangs, which reduced the numbers within the gang. Also, Community Resources Against Street

Hoodlums (CRASH), a specialized unit of the Los Angeles Police Department (LAPD) was tasked with combating gang-related crime. The unit was established in the South Central district of Los Angeles, California, United States, to combat rising gang violence during the period. Each of the LAPD's 18 divisions had a CRASH unit assigned to it, whose primary goal was to suppress gang-related crimes in the city, which came about primarily from the increase in illegal drug trade, especially cocaine. The CRASH program had increased arrests.

The combination of enhanced police action and gang-on-gang killings had seriously reduced the potential leaders of their particular gang. This was the environment of the gang sect when Freddie and DeMarius returned after school. It wasn't rare that gang members left for a while, but most went to prison. As they returned from school, they still saw potential in the gang. They felt that the violence was counter-productive. They didn't want ongoing feuds to endanger their gang or themselves. The current leader at this time, Walter Narstead, aka BB Man, had also returned to the sect twelve months earlier from his 2nd prison term. BB Man had so many meanings of what his moniker meant that people just stayed with BB Man. LAPD viewed him as a spoon, as they viewed all the old timers (BB Man was 31) because he continued to stir up trouble. He would incite the younger members to random chaos including walk-up shootings, drive-by shootings and grabbing young girls raping and killing them. This was bringing all kinds of retribution to both the neighborhood and the gang members and their families.

Both DeMarius and Freddie still had a good number of loyal

friends within the gang, who were encouraging them to do something. It ultimately proved fatal for them. Freddie and DeMarius had progressed within gang infrastructure and now ruled a crew of Hoover Criminals.

Both were not opposed to violence, but wanted to have any and all violence be such that it didn't bring a mass retribution back on any of them. Thus, the removal of BB Man was orchestrated. The subtle part was not in the manner of death, but in the implication of who the murderers were. No one ever thought of Freddie, DeMarius or anyone in BB man's inner circle or their sect. BB Man was killed in a home invasion. His wife was killed, his children were killed, the dog was beaten to death and, before they left, the goldfish were spilled on the floor and stepped on. It was made clear that nothing was left alive in that house. It was also clear that this hit was made by the Columbians (their trademark assassination, yet no one could understand why they denied it because they were usually very proud of their work). Freeway Freddie chose this opportunity to not only lead a retaliation against the Columbians, but to seize leadership of the Hoover Crips. There was a hit on the Columbians, but all were wearing other gang's colors.

Freddie was the godfather of the Hoover Crips and DeMarius was co-Godfather. They had earned their titles as much by subtlety as by overt killing. They were not unwilling to stimulate acts of violence but had learned that violence stimulated retaliatory violence and, thus, became unpredictable. They had lost three of his trusted lieutenants over three years ago in unrelated drive-bys and began to work on alternative activities that still gave the gold, but did not allow the level of violence that endangered his lieutenants and, ultimately, himself.

Freddie got the idea from one of the city councilmen, Arlington Johnson. He suggested that the city pay the gangs not to put graffiti on walls, signs, or buildings. The councilman was expectedly laughed off.

However, when T-bone Thompson, the gang's procuring specialist, came in into Freddie's office to give both DeMarius and Freddie updates on deliveries laughing at the phone company as they were trying to recruit some of the "Baby gangsters" to work in a project with the telephone companies' Community Relations Team to paint out recent graffiti as telephone people would work with members of the community, especially the younger members, the idea solidified.

Kane saw a brilliant way of expanding his drug distribution channel and improving his communication. He arranged a meeting with DeMarius, who posed as a reformed gang member, one who had become sick of the killing and violence, and the local city councilman, Arlington Johnson. Johnson had represented South Central Los Angeles for 38 years and had seemed to improve the lot of quite a few of his constituents.

Actually, many had benefited from Johnson's efforts, but when they could, they moved out of the council district. There had been a continuing migration of the Black community, if not out of Watts, at least out to the west to Inglewood and beyond. Watts' population now was about one-fourth Hispanic, many of which had been included under recent amnesty laws. Still, there were about 500,000 illegal migrants in the Los Angeles basin who were afraid of the program, or didn't understand it, or had entered the

US after the amnesty date.

DeMarius was quickly remembered as the little boy who had lost his mother years ago by Councilman Johnson. Freddie Kane was counting on it. He told DeMarius, "You would be catnip to this guy." Johnson was unaware of DeMarius's trusted position in the Hoover Criminals, but was more than willing to support a reformed gang member and his re-entry to society. DeMarius had indicated that there were several, some 20 in number, that were interested in getting real jobs yet wanted to be able to be role models in the community. DeMarius suggested that the telephone company offered jobs that could offer good pay and be able to provide high profile jobs for potential role models. DeMarius also suggested that Johnson meet with Kane to ensure that the Hoover Crips would not retaliate against the people in this program. Johnson had worked furiously with executives of Pacific Bell to agree to this program and, also, with the Los Angeles Police Department to get agreement for starting the 'Bright Lights' program.

The 'Bright Lights' program called for Pacific Bell to employ and train some 20 of the former gang members in telephone craft jobs, working in central offices and outside plant positions. The name originated from a variation of President Bush's famous "thousand points of light" or, as some cynics suggested, this was the only light at the end of the tunnel.

The meeting between Johnson and Freddie was orchestrated to make Freddie a victim of the system, one who has worked in his own way to better the community. In fact, several businesses in the district that employed over 250 people had been financed by Freddie. Freddie neglected to point out that not only had the original financing come from the sale of cocaine, but many of his business concerns were thinly veiled money laundering fronts. However, Johnson was desperate to show his constituency some progress against the gangs and received tacit approval to lessen police surveillance on the Hoover Crips in return for the gang's agreement to not retaliate against 'Bright Lights' members.

It took about six months for the media exposure to wane; it took nearly as long for gang members to go through the training. It began with considerable training in refining basic reading skills and in refining talking without streetwise jargon. The Hoover Crips had actually paid for an additional tutor to accelerate this part of the process.

It was during this period after training that these people were working generally alone with remote supervision and, in some cases, were given more responsibility or different hours. The evening shift was generally not as busy and allowed for some interesting activities. Members in the central office would monitor the lines of other gangs' leaders, fellow gang members (Freddie was not going to be "overthrown" like his predecessors), and favorite public phones accessed by the police, concerned about their radios being monitored. It was this "improved" communication that enhanced Freddie's reputation. He always seemed to be "in the know."

But the real surprise was the distribution channel that the telephone company inadvertently provided. Fellow employees scared to buy "on the street" would pay premium prices to get a "safe buy." The fear of buying on the street raised the concern of bad shit, narcs, and getting robbed or shot. These were generally social users whose habits were not daily routines. Over a year's time,

'Bright Lights' had introduced over 700 new "clients," as DeMarius called them.

Freddie Kane was certainly furious at DeMarius, not just for ripping off the drug sales money but for not being where he was supposed to be when the explosion occurred. He asked Crazy Lester who was used for the hit.

"What was those names?"

"It was Fat Mikey and Rabbit. They did just what we asked them to do."

"I want them lit up by some boys in red bandanas. Then I want them to do a drive-by to the Compton Piros. Then send T-Loc over to drop a dime with the 'Ros that Fat Mikey and Rabbit did the drive-by. Give the Bloods their address."

"Why not just shoot them?" asked Crazy Lester.

Kane smiled. "Because I don't want any of the cuzz to know that we're doin' 'em. And I don't want DeMarius to know that I know he's skimming."

"Hey, righteous. DeMarius will think that it's just the crazy Bloods tryin' to smoke our deal. And Mikey and Rabbit won't be around to tell the homeboys."

GOD IS IN THE DETAILS

The next morning, Bo went directly to the telephone garage where Terry Simpson had worked. He had dropped Jenny at her house, telling her to take it easy in the morning and not come into work if she didn't want to. Jenny said she would come in in the late afternoon, and gave Bo the password to her computer so that he could access the files he needed for his investigation. But he could have easily guessed—it was her son's name.

When Bo got to the garage, he used Jenny's desk and computer to get the background information for Terry. He knew that there often were details in any incident that gave insight to the "why" of an incident. These details would be of interest to Healy, but the company was only interested in elements that would reflect badly on the company.

Bo typed in Jenny's son's name—"Josiah"—and then began to access several programs. He made copies of a number of files and put them in a folder on his thumb drive for later review. Later, when he went home, he would send all the information he had gotten so far to John Healy.

His day was full, as he was asked to give an update in person to his boss on all aspects of Terry Simpson. He also had an appointment in the afternoon with a District Manager and his team about an employee who had been stealing company equipment. Finally, that night he was having a family dinner at Duncan Barrett's house.

Bo was thinking as he drove to the District Manager's office in the Wilshire District. The address was 4201 Wilshire Blvd. He thought it was peculiar that all buildings were generally referred to by their address number only. 818 (full address: 818 W. 7th Street) was Marketing's building. 420 (420 Grand) housed the Central Office equipment. 740 (740 S. Olive) was the Regional HQ location. He arrived at 4201 and parked underneath in some "Company Car" reserved spots. The building was not fully utilized by the telephone company. It was actually marked "Carnation Company", for the Carnation Milk brand. It housed the milk company's business office and some executive offices. Bo remembered that all the business offices had no public face. No one wanted disgruntled customers coming into offices directly.

☦

The last time he was at this building was following an incident where an ex-boyfriend came into the office brandishing a gun. Bo was called out as he was one of the few investigators who had a conceal carry permit. He was two blocks away, so he actually beat the police there.

Bo thought as he entered that this was a lot like his Iraq training, but worse in that there were literally 100 innocents. When he reached the floor where the incident was unfolding, he saw a woman dressed in a navy blazer, red blouse and white skirt with blue and white spectacles, quietly waving frantically at him. She whispered, "A man somehow got by the door code. He was holding a gun in his hand, not pointing it and not anxious or disturbed. I have been hustling folks out as best I can. I got thirty out, but 20 remain, including Lois Burnett, one of my supervisors. I think the other 20 are frozen in fear. I also think that Lois is why he's here."

"How are you so calm?" Bo asked.

"I was a cop… until I was shot. I really don't need this shit today."

"It's okay, I got it," Bo replied, thinking, "I got what?"

He started in the office, which was a large bullpen with several four-foot-high partitions separating groups of 6-8 desks. He looked and counted only five people standing. He assumed the rest had hit the ground hiding. He snuck along the wall to secure an approach that was behind the man. He was one partition and about twelve feet away, with his weapon in his hand, when the woman he assumed was Lois Burnett yelled, "What?" Lois was about 5'9" and maybe 170 pounds, but you would never consider her fat or even overweight. She emitted a sense of power and strength that was apparent. Less than a second later, Lois struck the man in his throat. He dropped the gun, grabbed his throat with both hands and fell to his knees. Bo moved to get the gun immediately. Lois took a chair, kicked the man to his back and jammed the chair over him, successfully pinning his hands, shoulder and head.

She then calmly sat down on the chair and, in the most menacing voice that Bo could remember since his mother went face-to-face with that nun at his elementary school, said, "Do you want to say that again?"

Bo could see the man shaking "No" with his whole body.

The police arrived shortly afterward. Bo had put the gun in a baggie and identified himself as security. Officer Billy Jenkins was alone and looked twelve years old. Bo put his company ID and his conceal permit on the desk. He announced that he was carrying and then narrated that he was slowly taking his weapon from the holster on his right hip with left finger and thumb and also laid it on the desk. Bo felt in more danger during this than he had when he first entered the office.

Additional officers arrived and the sergeant took over. He had been briefed quickly by Betty Spironi.

"You the company security guy?" he asked.

Bo said, "Yes."

The sergeant turned to Billy, "You can holster your weapon, Billy," and a few seconds of no movement went by. "NOW, Billy." Then Billy holstered his weapon. "It's OK, Billy, I would have yelled at you more if you hadn't secured the scene."

Looking back at Bo, he said, "You seemed to have gotten this well under control."

"No, not really. Lois was the one who brought down the intruder," Bo said, nodding at the woman sitting a few feet away.

"Really?" said the sergeant.

"Really, and I suggest you be polite in your interview," Bo smiled.

Later, Bo introduced himself to Lois.

"I saw you coming up from behind. I was trying to keep his focus on me," Lois said.

"Who was he?" Bo asked.

"He thought he was an old boyfriend. We went on one date that lasted 45 minutes and it was for dinner. I never ate so fast."

"What did he say that made you yell?" Bo asked.

Lois replied, "He said he felt disrespected by me as a girlfriend. Then, he said that he didn't realize I was so fat."

"You're kidding!"

"That's what I thought, then I got mad."

"You saved a lot of people from getting hurt. I consider you a hero."

Lois smiled, "The sergeant said the same thing." Then with a raised eyebrow, "He looks like boyfriend material."

"He'd be lucky!"

"Damn straight!" Lois walked toward the sergeant.

☦

Bo was smiling at the memory. The district manager office was on the floor above the business office. Offices in telephone company buildings had strict space, furniture and amenities outlined in several guidebooks. One volume was called Bell System Practices and one was called System Instructions. These books outlined several things—safety practices, installation and repair practices, office sizes, door lettering, type of tiles for flooring and carpets (and who got carpet and what kind). These books were not only venerated within the company, but were respected as the gold standard for large organizations. The US Army had used these practices to set up their guidebooks.

But when office space was rented, the guidebook was suspended. Bo entered the conference room that was as large as three conference rooms in his building. The table was 16 feet long surrounded by 12 leather chairs. As Bo sat in the chair, he wanted to take it home, it was so comfortable.

He had been guided to his seat. There were three other men besides the district manager. He was sitting directly across from Bo and introduced himself as Victor Kaufman. Bo knew he had been with the company 12 years and had recently been promoted. He also knew from the setting, the seating, and the number of participants that there was an agenda that he did not yet know.

He also introduced his "team", but it felt like he was saying "Larry, Mo and Curly Joe—the Three Stooges." They nodded, but said nothing.

Bo had been working on this for a couple of months. Ramon Martinez had been stealing and installing telephone gear in exchange for clothing. It turned out that Ramon had a girlfriend—and a wife. The clothing had been for the girlfriend, because he couldn't get access to his banking money because his wife controlled the money. So, he used "gifts" to woo his new love. The early information came from a repair tech who was asked to repair equipment that was not on the telephone records. Records were not always correct, but the customer told the tech he was stupid several times and several different ways. So, he passed along the discrepancy to the business office. They had passed it to security and, ultimately, to Bo.

It turned out that there were three different businesses with a similar issue. It also turned out that Ramon had been recently at these businesses on a repair or installation visit. All the businesses could not really deny what had happened. Two of them said they did pay, just not in cash. One business owner was not aware and was really being duped by his own office manager. Bo had asked if he would be willing to set up a sting. He was more than thrilled to do this.

The sting had worked perfectly. Bo had pictures of equipment that had been marked in the storeroom, pictures of the equipment being carried up the external stairs of the customer's location by Ramon, and pictures of Ramon 10 minutes later carrying an armful of ladies' dresses and blouses.

"We understand that you have found one of our techs has been careless with telephone company equipment," Victor started.

"We believe this is theft, not carelessness," Bo replied.

"What evidence do you have?"

Bo was not going to show all his cards immediately.

He took a couple of sheets out that showed the first theft. "Here is the telephone equipment that was at this clothing business that was not on our records."

Victor snorted, "You think there are never errors in our records? How naïve are you, Mr. Connecticut?" He smiled and shared his disdain with his 'team'.

Bo knew then that he was going to hear "Bozo" in the next minute or two.

"Here is the dispatch record of Ramon Martinez." Bo offered

the sheet.

"Again, that doesn't prove anything. What a Bozo you are!"

"Right on time," Bozo thought.

Another sheet. "Here is a signed affidavit of the customer saying that he traded women's clothing for telco equipment."

Victor flinched a little in his chair. "Well, he could have gotten the equipment another way and is using Ramon as a defense. This appears very circumstantial."

Too many Law and Order episodes, Bo thought. He smiled to himself as he prepared to look unsure of himself and presented a second customer.

"We have a second customer that had unauthorized equipment and Ramon at the premises twice," Bo said.

"This looks like a witch hunt, Connecticut," Victor said, raising his voice.

"And here is a second customer with his signed affidavit."

"You have found two customers that have illicit equipment and know of Ramon because he was there on a legitimate visit. You're using his name as a scapegoat."

"I have a third customer as well," Bo countered.

"Okay, there is obviously a conspiracy against Ramon constructed by someone who doesn't like him," said Victor with complete assurance.

"I don't understand. This is clear evidence that he has done this multiple times. We believe there is more," Bo said. "Why are you defending him?"

"Because we are like a family in this district and don't look for ways to hang any of our team out to dry. We prefer to talk with the person as well," Victor said.

"You don't believe any of this?" Bo asked.

"No, we don't," Victor said firmly.

"Okay. Here is a picture of some equipment in your telco closet. Note the date. Here is Ramon carrying the equipment up the stairs to this customer. Here."

Bo stopped as Victor interrupted: "How do you know it is the same equipment?"

Bo then laid out another picture. "Here is a picture at the customer premise of the equipment. Note the date, time and same serial numbers."

Victor remained quiet.

"Here is a picture leaving the same stairs minutes later carrying ladies' clothing," Bo said.

"How do we know that this is Ramon?" Victor offered with less bravado.

"Here are signed affidavits from the customer, one of my associates—the cameraman incidentally—and myself. My associate and my affidavit detail following Ramon from the garage on Olympic to the customer premises where he received the clothing, and then to a residential address (not his home) and then to the garage."

Bo continued, "Why are you not accepting this? Have you talked with Ramon about this?"

Victor and the two others looked at the man on Bo's left—who Bo called Mo. Victor turned back to Bo and said, "I don't think so."

Then, Bo asked with a song in his heart, "Are there others involved with this?" with his hands wide enough to include everyone at the table.

Victor stuttered, "No… No… N… N… No," with a glare at Mo.

"Finally, just so you know, we have a signed affidavit from the girlfriend indicating that Ramon had given her over 100 outfits. She reluctantly agreed to return all the items. Ramon needs to be terminated by 5:00 pm tomorrow. We are not sure if the police will pursue this further."

Victor said, "I am not sure we can get that done by tomorrow."

Bo calmly answered, "You had better, Victor. You wouldn't want to look like a Bozo! Thank you, gentlemen."

It was 3:45 pm. He smiled, thinking that he could get to the family dinner early by 4:30.

BETTER THAN MCJOBS

Arlington Johnson sat in his home office as Bo drove to dinner. Arlington was reflecting on how hard it was to really have a significant impact on the inner city. There were successes. But most often, the success was that you got out. Very few had stayed to help rebuild or recruit. Magic Johnson had invested in a major 12-screen multiplex in Baldwin Hills, providing some significant jobs for people. Arlington thought about his 'Bright Lights' program that he helped spearhead, but even it was getting some shady rumors.

Arlington had been on the city council for 36 years—never mayor, but maybe he was more powerful than some of the mayors. He was street smart and street tough. He had shrunk a little as he had gotten older, even from his 5'6" frame that had been an All-City point guard at Jefferson High School. He got a scholarship to USC and was a good player—started his junior and senior year—but his 5'6" stature became dwarfed (not his favorite word) by ever-increasing numbers of incredibly gifted athletes that were 6'4" and taller.

Arlington had stayed in the community after college. He worked several city government jobs that let him be of service, helping people fight the bureaucracy of permits, licenses, etc. But maybe because the scope was limited, or, maybe because he wanted some recognition, he had been seduced by the call of politics. He worked on others' campaigns—starting out part time and then full time. Those he helped would say, "Johnson can get out the vote."

It was hard to be in politics that long and not be smeared with scandal, corruption, or be viewed in some jaded fashion. Arlington had been rather successful in this, however. Not perfect, but successful more so than not. He still lived in the same house where he was born. His mother still lived with him. His father had been killed by a drunk driver when he was five years old. He had memories of his father, but he couldn't tell if they were his own memories or memories of his mother's stories about his father.

Arlington would buy a car, maintain it impeccably, and drive it for twelve years. He never wanted to embarrass his mother. She was religious but not fanatical. When she described her feelings about God, her gratitude for her life, her husband, her son, and her work as a teacher to young children, Arlington felt like he had met a God that was much bigger than any God he had met in church. They had changed churches a couple of times—usually after Mom determined that "the preacher had gotten too big for his britches." Arlington saw as much politics in the various churches than he did at City Hall. He told his Mom that there was less hypocrisy at City Hall.

When Arlington had been accused publicly in a paternity suit, his mother knew that it was wrong. It wasn't that Arlington had not had girlfriends. He had two loves of his life—one moved away in eighth grade; one had been killed in another drunk driving accident in college. Arlington had stopped drinking then. He occasionally had "a woman friend"—as his mother called it—but she knew he would never deny a child. As it turned out, the woman filing the paternity suit hadn't even been pregnant. Arlington was in as close an election as he ever experienced, and believed that this was somehow politically motivated. Ironically, his poll numbers improved both at the "leak" in the press and the revelation of it being bogus. He won the election easily.

About six years ago, he had been working on anti-gang initiatives. There were gangs in his day, and he had been threatened if he didn't join a gang. Arlington said to all the gang "invitations" that came his way, "You guys are threatening me, but my mother would certainly kill me if I joined." Almost all the gang members had been taught by Mrs. Mary Johnson and still were moderately afraid of her. His mom had encouraged him. In fact, she was the best advisor he had. Eventually, his basketball celebrity had kicked in and had protected him from this type of pressure.

He got a coffee from the Keurig, which he thought was the best invention second only to Dr. Pepper. Then went to the living room where his mother usually sat, either reading or looking out to the neighborhood. Today, he noticed a book in her hands and her eyes on the neighborhood.

"Good afternoon, Mama." Arlington smiled.

"What's up, sweetheart?" Knowing they would be talking for a while, she closed her book.

Arlington smiled more broadly. His mom, no matter who she was talking with, would put aside everything in front of her and focus on the speaker, giving her full attention. Arlington had always felt more important no matter what was discussed. He was truly blessed with her in his life. So were many others.

"I am feeling a little inadequate right now. I am getting some feedback or rumors about the 'Bright Lights' program," he said. There was no answer, but her eyes were right on his. He continued, "Some of the political input is that I put some distance between it and me. Some say in the community that it is not all good. No specifics."

"Baby, do you remember when you first started some of your 'ideas'?"

"Of course!"

"What was the one before 'Bright Lights'?" she asked.

"I had suggested the city pay the gangs to not have graffiti all over the neighborhood. It was generally ridiculed by both gangs and police," Arlington said.

Mary asked, "Do you remember what I said?"

"I remember exactly—'Ar, that is just silly!'"

"What else?" she prompted.

"I don't remember."

"I asked you if you had a better idea, and you said, 'No,' then I said you should promote that idea."

"It didn't get any traction at all," he replied.

"Not true—you told me that a reformed gang member approached you with another idea—to provide alternative jobs better than working at McDonald's. The telephone company was one of the partners in his program. There have been 30 new jobs every year with the telephone company—frame attendants, technicians, service reps—all jobs that paid significantly more than fast food service, and had health benefits, vacations, and a dignity in the work. So far over half of the graduates had continued to work for the telephone company, and the program was deemed a success." Mary continued, "So why all the down thoughts now?"

"Mom, the negative feedback feels right somehow," Arlington said.

"Ar, do you know anyone not in politics, not in the community, that could give you a perspective?"

Arlington remembered meeting with a security guy some years ago, who might have or be able to have some real information. His name was somewhat remarkable.

Arlington blurted out, "Bozo!" and then, "Thanks, Mom." He almost ran back to his office.

※

Arlington had met Bo in his office about three years before. One of the people in the 'Bright Lights' program had disconnected his girlfriend's phone after he found out she was cheating on him. This was a fireable offense. He had accessed company records for her cable and pair information, used his telephone truck to get to the pole, and disconnected her service. However, the employee was good in every other aspect of the job. The management didn't want to fire him.

An executive suggested that if Arlington would sponsor this person, it could give him another chance—except nobody wanted to be "caught" working with Arlington directly because the company didn't want to be viewed as having political connections. Management felt that a visit by the security office could be justified from review later on. Bo had won the visit assignment.

After a brief introduction, Arlington said to Bo, "I would not ask you to do anything wrong."

"I wouldn't do anything improper," Bo smiled.

Then they sat for about ten seconds looking at each other and simultaneously burst into laughter. Arlington got up and went to a mini-fridge and pulled out two Dr. Pepper's.

"I found out in school that their pitch of having a Dr. Pepper at ten, two, and four was a strategy that focused on non-lunch and dinner times. They didn't think that they could compete with Coke at mealtimes. So they focused on other times," Bo said.

Johnson took a long swig straight from the bottle.

"I have always liked the underdog, so I keep it here for every time I laugh. I go through a case a week."

They talked about other things—being raised by single mothers, God- (but not church-) influenced homes and Bo's son (who Arlington could tell was a missing piece in Bo's life). Bo shared the story of his fight with Rick Francis in fifth grade, and his mother's protecting him.

"What a great mom story!" Arlington said.

Arlington cited his mom's protection as well. The two men felt a connection because they both were raised by such loving and watchful mothers.

Arlington continued, "That's great. We all need a little protection from time to time. I will stand up for this boy. I hope you can look at this incident objectively."

Bo smiled. "I will investigate this thoroughly tomorrow and I expect to find insufficient evidence for any further action. Nice to meet you, Councilman."

Arlington stood and looked at the closed door and smiled for a full five minutes, then went to the mini-fridge for another Dr. Pepper.

A HOUSE IS NOT A HOME

Bo was anxious to see Jimmy. His son had broken his arm last year and was wondering if it would have any impact on this baseball season. Jimmy loved baseball, as did Bo, and they would play with a bat and tennis ball on the street in front of the house until after dark during the summer. As a result, Jimmy had the softest hands of any fielder Bo had ever seen. But he could tell the arm was not yet 100% when he saw Jimmy throw the ball. Jimmy had broken his arm while skateboarding last summer. He observed a tentative approach to going all out.

But now it was soccer season, where Jimmy gave "all out" new meaning. Bo thought that Jimmy had time to heal physically and mentally before the season started.

"You are really getting back to your Jimmy-level!" Bo said as Jimmy smiled.

Bo also reflected on his family's living arrangements. Gloria and Jimmy lived in the guest house on a triple lot in Studio City. The hacienda-style home had several buildings on the property. It had been custom built by Duncan Barrett, a retired actor, who was still relatively young, in his mid-50s, but who had retired ten years earlier after a very successful show where he played the partner of Lady Cop, which starred a long-time beauty as a police detective. The show ran for 12 years and made Duncan wealthy. He had wisely managed his money through real estate and the stock market and had tripled his net worth since his retirement from acting.

Duncan remained active in animal rights and police charities. He wore the same clothes every day—a signature outfit of khaki slacks with a blue button-down shirt, with sleeves rolled up to just below the elbow. Bo thought that Duncan must have ten of the exact same outfits, because he was always impeccable. The creases of his slacks were always sharp as knives, his shirts looked like they had been pressed while he was wearing them—yet at the same time, his look seemed incredibly relaxed.

Even more remarkable were Duncan's two black Labradors—Gladys and Knight—who either stood or sat next to him like bookends. Knight had a severe drooling issue and was currently wiping his mouth on Bo's pants.

"How come Knight never does this to you?" Bo asked.

Seeming oblivious that his dogs would do anything untoward, Duncan said, "Do what to me? Bo, nice to see you," Duncan replied.

They were interrupted by Jimmy yelling "Yes, he's here!" coming through the patio before Bo could answer.

"Yes, I am." Bo smiled as he hugged his son.

TWISTED PAIR

Gloria followed Jimmy in and said hello, and then went to the kitchen to make dinner. Duncan had known Bo's mother, Winifred "Win" Connecticut for years. They had met in AA and, like everyone else, he fell in love with her upon meeting her. Duncan had remained sober for over 20 years. Win had "slips" that broke her continuous sobriety, but she, as they called it, "kept coming back." As far as Bo knew, their love was platonic. Duncan was such a gentleman that he would never say, and Bo had no desire to know anyway.

†

It turned out that Duncan had other reasons for accommodating Gloria and Jimmy. One late night, only Duncan, Bo, Gladys and Knight were up.

It was a moderate summer night and Bo said, "Duncan, we cannot thank you enough for letting Gloria and Jimmy stay with you. I know my mother also appreciates you doing this as well."

Duncan yawned and said, "Bo, that's not the only reason I'm doing this. Very few people know I was adopted. My adoptive parents were good people, but I think they thought having a child would be different. It wasn't that they were ever mean, but their expression of love was providing good food, good lodging and a good education. I don't remember ever being hugged. No one said, 'I love you.'"

"I left home at 17 to join the Navy. I got caught lying on the form about my age and was bounced out. At 18, I signed up again."

Duncan paused and said, "Your family gushes more love than Knight has drool."

Bo noted the first awareness of Knight's affliction.

Duncan said, "You have provided me with the family I wanted all my life."

Bo knew that Duncan loved his family and for the past four years had provided housing for Gloria and Jimmy at no cost. A series of events had caused this arrangement. Gloria had become increasingly worried about what Bo did for a living. After Bo almost being shot on the job, Win driving Jimmy while she was drunk, and an anxiety attack on Gloria's part basically ended their marriage, they had stayed married for insurance purposes but were man and wife for no other reason—except for Jimmy. Neither said anything derogatory about the other to Jimmy. They remained partners in parenting him.

Duncan had offered Bo's family the solution of staying with him, and they took him up on it temporarily, but Bo's financial limitations and the love that developed for Duncan with Jimmy and Gloria let the situation morph into a more permanent solution.

The "almost shooting" occurred when Bo went to an employee's house when the employee was on disability to ask him about "disappearing furniture" at one of the garage locations. It was a small case with little significance, and Bo was just gathering information. He had called the employee to make an appointment. After knocking, he was greeted by a short, obese man who held a gun pointed straight at Bo's face and pulled the trigger two seconds after opening the door. Nothing happened—it turns out, the chamber was empty—and Bo immediately struck the man in the throat two times. The man dropped the gun and fell. Bo tied his arms behind his back and tied his feet together using the drapes cords he tore down, then called 911. After calling the cops, Bo went to the bathroom and threw up. It turned out that the man had mis-administered his medication and then highlighted it with some bourbon. He had been on the verge of committing suicide but had only been coherent enough to put three bullets in the chamber. The first was empty and the second shot was a dry fire. Bo didn't want to think about what the next trigger pull would have been.

"Wild Bill" had urged all Special Agents to get a concealed carry weapon license upon joining the special agents, but Bo was tired of the pressure that came with carrying a gun from his time as an MP. However, Bo applied for his concealed carry permit on the way home that afternoon. When he got home and told Gloria, she wanted him to quit his job immediately and refused to have a gun in her house. Bo kept the gun in the trunk of his car.

Shortly after this, Win Connecticut had been asked by Gloria to pick up Jimmy after little league practice. She had been distracted by a call from a friend and Jimmy had fallen asleep in the car. She had parked the car in the driveway and went into the house still on the call. Later, she remembered about Jimmy and went out to the car and woke him up, taking him into the house. Jimmy was unaware: he saw nothing that indicated his grandmother had left him in the car. When Gloria got home and Win shared what had happened, Gloria went crazy. She did not want the woman ever to be in the house or to see Jimmy again. Bo told her firmly that he was not going to banish his mother from his son.

All of these things led to a "trial separation" that evolved into the current "temporary housing."

There had been "understandings." Gloria wanted no sex with Bo, which had been an unstated rule for the previous two years. She had wanted access to her son limited for Bo only, but Bo's refusal and Duncan (who had become close to Gloria), Jimmy and the therapist's urging had negated that rule. What evolved was a sometimes-comfortable truce between loving mother and father as far as Jimmy was concerned. Gloria was excellent financially. She had always managed the family's budget well. Selling the house and having rent-free living had given enough money for Bo's rent and living expenses. Neither were people who spent a lot of money. They had actually saved over $100,000 in the past few years.

Bill Martini, a steady participant in Sunday dinner for the last two years, had joined the family at 5:30 and sat between Bo's Mom and Gloria. Dinner was not only without incident but was full of laughter, as Bo talked about the folks in his office and the recent meeting with Vincent Kaufman.

After dinner, Bo and Bill talked about their jobs and how they had joined the Telephone Company because it felt like they were doing a job of service, similar to what they felt in the Army. It was still work and wasn't perfect. Bo's mom always said, "With work, they have to pay you. If it is fun, you have to pay them." They talked about the uneasy feeling of losing the jobs amid all the rumors of layoffs.

Bill Martini was supposed to have been driving for the Marketing Vice President the night that the repair technician had been blown up, but had gotten someone else to take the overtime because he was increasingly irritated by the manner of the 'Bright Lights' poster boy's attitude toward the Vice President. It was not so much that the Marketing VP was such a nice guy, but DeMarius acted as if he owned him. He even had adopted the strange phenomena of acting as if the driver, a term that Bill much preferred over chauffeur, was deaf, dumb, and invisible. Bill was scheduled tonight to do the same duty but had gotten someone to cover for him.

His job had never been one under any budget restraint. There was not even fear of losing the job like there was for every other telephone job due to restructure, reorganization, or re-engineering. Almost everyone understood it intellectually, and almost no one understood it emotionally. About 70 percent of all employees were between the ages of 40 and 50. The vast majority were white males, but the company had initiated a strong affirmative action program. Bill had seen that the Army also may have had gender bias, but war had a way of killing soldiers without bias.

Because of the dominance of the white males in the demographics of the targeted group, very few saw that this was really relatively fairly administered as regards to ethnicity. Bill and Bo both laughed thinking that an 80% population that was white male with gray hair was considered fair and equitable.

But it didn't really matter, because "fair" and "equitable" were not really consoling words when you lost your job. What made it worse was that almost everyone who lost their job had only ever worked for the telephone company. Many had parents, uncles, brothers that worked for the telephone company. They had planned to retire after thirty years or longer. The old company newsletters revered job longevity by highlighting those with service anniversaries. Now they were "lovers scorned" after giving the best years of their life to the company.

This led to almost a hysterical level of dysfunction. The people with attitude problems got worse. Then when it became clear that the attitude (or even speaking out in opposition to a policy, direction, or opinion of whomever was in power for the moment) would get your name on a list you didn't want to be on, or off a list you wanted to be on, everyone (not just the attitude cases) adopted a "hunker down" approach. While the companies were breaking new ground for increasing communication technically, one of the major companies providing communications just stopped doing it. This wasn't true for everyone, but many had secret frustrations and were counting their days until retirement or hoping for a special offer to incentivize them to leave early. One of the unanticipated results of the special offer incentives was that the company lost some of its best people. The offer was aimed at getting the deadwood out of the company. These were people who had either been bad for a long time with the company or had been identified as "bell-shaped" and not very flexible. They also could be from a group who had the temerity to question any comments from the officers. Legend had it that the President, with the squirrel face after a communication session with one of the geographical teams, called the executive vice president to tell him to get one of the team members out of the company from the corporate jet. Not long afterwards, the individual left the company.

Simultaneously, they were introducing teams to improve work processes that sometimes immediately caused the creative team members their jobs. This added to the dysfunction.

Still, Bill Martini thought his position was secure. It was secure for two reasons. One, the officers were not going to drive themselves. Two, an incident about fifteen years ago found an officer getting into an accident in Las Vegas (not Pacific Bell's territory) with a female employee who was not his wife. Everything could have been taken care of, except the officer was drunk, and the vehicle was a company car. The solution then—as it remained now—was to have drivers always take the officers. Bill enjoyed the job and really did keep the counsel of most of his passengers.

The exception was that he sometimes shared things about the President and the Vice President of Marketing with his best friend, Bo Connecticut. Bill was scheduled to be the driver tonight but had gotten someone to cover for him. Instead of listening to the megalomaniac chatter of DeMarius, Bill could spend the evening with Bo, Gloria, Jimmy, Duncan and Bo's absolutely crazy mother.

He did need to talk with Bo, but tonight was not the night.

THEY DON'T LOCK YOU UP
FOR BEING CRAZY

Bo got up and sat on the edge of the bed after pressing the alarm. It was the fifth buzz of the snooze alarm but the first that he had sat up for. He looked down and kicked at the pile of clothes at his feet. He figured that socks worn less than ten hours could be repeated. He grabbed his black shoes, went to the drawer, and grabbed undershorts and a Penney's T-shirt. Bo checked the armpits to see if they were yellow. He hated how it looked when guys would hold their hands behind their heads and display two yellow armpits. It was his big concession to cleanliness.

It wasn't that he minded cleaning up, but since he was alone, the need was not that great. He shaved in the shower. He always thought that it would be great to get a non-fogging mirror, but could only remember it when he was in the shower.

Spending time with Jenny made him think of Gloria. Thinking of Gloria made him irritated. One of his favorite pastimes was to make a list of all the things that pissed him off about her. He'd always start with sex, add her bitching about his work, and then top it with her complaint about not having enough money (which it wasn't even true as their savings had continued to grow.) She could make him feel "less than" faster than anybody or anything. "Less than" was the psychologist's words. Therapy had cost him about $1500 for the 50% that the insurance didn't cover. If the psychologist had been just a marriage counselor, the 50% wouldn't have been covered.

Somewhere while making the list, he would begin to list the good things about Gloria, like being a loving mother, a pretty good friend when she wasn't a bitch, and being absolutely beautiful. Maybe Bill Martini was right; maybe he did still love her. But he didn't think he was in love with her anymore. He had taken no action on divorce since moving out eleven months ago. She made every arrangement possible for Bo to see his son, Jimmy. Bo thought she did that for two reasons: one, because they both knew he was a good and loving father, and Jimmy loved being with his Dad, and two, Bo would have filed formal divorce papers if anything would have prevented him from seeing his son.

Bo finished up his Grape Nuts and began cleaning up the kitchen. He liked Grape Nuts since they seemed to be eternally fresh, or maybe they tasted the same when they were stale. It did concern him as he tried to clean Monday's bowl because the Grape Nuts dried inside seemed like dried concrete. In fact, yesterday's bowl needed Bon-Ami to get it clean enough for the dishwasher. He finished cleaning up the one-bedroom apartment by kicking the clothes and shoes on the floor near his bed into the closet and closing the door. One final look around, and he could see it was all right for when Jimmy came over tonight.

☦

Bo met in Katie Fischer's office. Katie was the Director of External Affairs and was also responsible for any media interface. Katie also was a classmate of Bo's from 1st grade through high school. She dated Bill Martini throughout their junior year. She was pretty, smart, and willing to fall in love at any time. Unfortunately, she was equally willing to fall out of love at any time. She had been married and divorced three times but had a son and a daughter with husband #2—her longest marriage of four years.

They became friends in fourth grade. She said, "I like the way you defended your mom. You can be my friend… but never my boyfriend." It was a little awkward when she was dating Bo's best friend, Bill, but he wanted to keep both friends, so even if Bill and Katie hated each other, he decided that he wasn't required to hate either of them. It didn't last long, as Katie soon found another boyfriend and Bill shifted into just a friend.

The friendship of all three became cemented in Iraq. Katie had gone to college and joined ROTC, which helped her expenses, but also placed her in Iraq at the same time as Bo and Bill. Katie was assigned as a First Lieutenant in the Intelligence group. A sergeant had approached her regarding the smuggling of antiquities out of Iraq by one of the contract companies. She wanted Bill and Bo to help her verify what she had been told.

Bill Martini had secured a nondescript, rusted Toyota, allowing them to drive through several streets without notice, either from the contractor or any Iraqis. They had followed one of the contractors over a 2-month period, securing photos and detailed locations of transfer points. It was clear that there were several pieces of gold and silver treasures.

After several nights in burkas and robes with the excitement of potential danger, they took the evidence to the local Army CID person. After he chastised all of them, especially Bo, as he should have known better, he said he would check it out. He did say something about Nancy Drew and the Hardy boys. They left all the evidence in a folder with the pictures.

Oddly, they didn't hear anything back for over a month. Katie went back to the office of CID and the agent she spoke with was no longer here. He had been transferred back to the states. The agent she spoke with said there was no file on this.

Katie told Bill and Bo, "The new agent looked at me like I was from another planet. He knew nothing about it and had checked both the computer files and the hard-copy files right in front of me."

"Did you ask where the previous agent went?" Bill asked.

"He told me that he was in Germany three weeks ago and was ordered here right away. There was no overlap at all and he didn't even know the name of the agent who left until yesterday when his boss had said it, but quickly changed the subject. His name was Eric Addley."

Katie continued, "He went on to say that he had been doing this for a long time and whatever this was, it was generally something the CIA was involved with, which made it overt or political.

I did nothing to follow up with him and I won't now. I asked a question about this. I have already gone from Germany to here and don't want to go to some other 'hell-hole.' No thanks – and I suggest you do nothing as well."

Bo said, "He gave you a lot of information that was very detailed and yet was cautious about doing anything. That doesn't make sense."

"I may have flirted a little. He seemed like he had potential, but I was so shocked about what he said that I left and called you guys."

"The next 'Mr. Katie'?" Bo asked.

"No, the next one would have followed up on the agent."

Bo said, "We should think about this for a bit. Any computer search might bring transfers to us all." They all agreed.

Two days later, Katie was called in to her CO's office and reamed for what she was doing. "You should have informed me before I got a call from the General saying my team is endangering any number of people."

Captain Stanley Brockton looked at Katie, actually took a suspicious look around his own office, like someone else was there listening and then said, "Look, Katie, I was just reamed for 30 minutes directly by my boss's boss's boss. They were bypassed completely. There will be no record of the discussion. Please don't see or talk to anybody about this. Is there anyone else aware of this?"

"No, I wanted to make sure I had something real first," Katie lied.

Brockton said, "Well, you don't. This conversation didn't happen. You are dismissed."

That night, Katie met with Bo and Bill. She told them about her meeting with Brockton.

She said, "Brockton is one of the straightest shooters I know. He does not shy away from things. But he was scared. I don't know what we could do now."

Bo said, "This obviously is above our pay grade. Katie, Brockton obviously thinks he is being watched. You should assume you are being watched as well. Also, we should assume that our phones are compromised." Bo continued, "We need to go out tonight, appear to get drunk saying out loud that you got yelled at from your boss, do not say why and say you just wanted to be with your friends from school and get soused. Then, we don't connect with each other in any way for at least six weeks. What we do know is Eric Addley was not the name of the CID agent. We should try to reach out to Michael Gonzales in about six weeks."

Bill asked, "Could we have been following a CIA agent the whole time?"

"We might have been endangering someone undercover. But does the CIA care about stolen antiquities?" Bo replied.

"We also know that your new 'potential' boyfriend either lied or was lied to. Don't take this wrong, but, Katie, I think you were being worked. I also bet any search for 'Eric Addley' will light up many screens. We won't be doing that."

Before the self-imposed six weeks of silence was done, all of them found themselves transferred to new next assignments in the states, but at separate postings. It would be years before they talked about this again. It no longer was an issue they needed to chase. Bo had shared, "It takes quite a bit of horsepower to make a CID disappear and transfer three friends out of the country in as short of time as six weeks."

Bo knew that it would remain in their thoughts.

But it wasn't front of mind today. There was the technician explosion to deal with.

Bo treasured his friendship with Katie and had gotten there early. Having a friend of the opposite sex, Bo thought, that you didn't ever sleep with was like having a guy on your side in the enemy camp. Sleeping with them changed the dynamic—they would never give up the details of the secret decoder ring, that code that explained women's thinking.

Katie would ask Bo, "What did Gloria say?"

Bo would answer and be given the right response. It always worked except with Gloria. She remained a mystery to both Katie and Bo.

"You look awful and tired," Katie greeted him.

"I am not awful, only tired."

"Something fun?" Katie asked with a wicked smile.

"Far from it, just got my sleep interrupted all night. First with heartburn, took a pill and was up for half an hour. Then the next door neighbor got home at 2:00 am and made enough noise so I was awake from 2 to 3. Then I woke up again at 4 with a knocking noise, I thought. What woke me was the alien in the sleeping bag on the floor next to my bed. He was sitting up—obviously he had heard the knocking too. You know how you blink when you see something that doesn't make sense. Well, I blinked long enough that he disappeared, but also long enough where you lose that sleepy fog that lets you go right back to sleep. My nightmares have a theatrical flavor."

Katie smiled again, "That did sound fun. You know the company has help for you."

Bo smiled. "You know they don't lock you up for being crazy, just for acting crazy. If you don't move, they don't know. How are you?"

Katie grinned sheepishly, "I may have met the next ex-husband."

Bo said, "I recommend living in sin for at least 1 year before your vows." They both laughed.

Others joined the meeting. The meeting was to update key personnel on investigation into the death of Terry Simpson. Also coming to the meeting was Bo's boss, Carol Dellamor, and someone from the company President's staff. Bo was to give them a summary of whatever police interface had occurred and of any developments in the investigation.

As he was reviewing his notes, he again saw that the original repair call had asked for a particular technician. He remembered seeing this, but had not discussed it with anyone. Bo wanted to think about this and research it more before sharing it with this group. He gave updates on informing the police detective, and gave his opinion that the technician's background suggested that it was not necessarily aimed at him and it was still too early to offer any conclusions at this time.

The meeting took 15 minutes.

☦

Bo Connecticut returned to his desk. He really liked his cubicle, four floors below Katie's office. It had a view out the north side of 1010 Wilshire, Pacific Bell's Los Angeles headquarters building, and treated him to a view of Dodger Stadium from its eighth-floor vantage point. However, there were about 20 days a year when the smog was so bad he could not see the Stadium or even the 76 sign on the Unocal building three blocks away. He also had vacant cubicles on both sides created by the most recent Management Income Protection Plan (MIPP), which gave long-timers a year's salary as a bonus to retire. Both investigators in the adjacent cubicles had taken the option, and no one had come to claim their offices.

Bo's cubicle sported a custom needlepoint done by Gloria in earlier, happier days. The needlepoint read:

> *The creator of Bozo the Clown is looking for potential clowns because he says only 25 licensed Bozos are working these days, down from 150.*
> *Unlicensed Bozos seem to be flourishing.*

The rest of the cubicle was unspectacular in every way. The desk was literally like a thousand other desks in this building, and the chair didn't match. The credenza, a status symbol for every second-level manager, also didn't match.

The levels of management were like the caste system of medieval times. The lowest level of management, the first level, was generally a supervisor of non-management or craft people. It also could be a staff position without subordinates or the lowest level professional, like an engineer. In the army, E-4 could be a Corporal or a Specialist 4. The second level was either a high-level professional or a supervisor of the first level. There was a further gradation in the second level referred to as high-band second level or low-band second level. There was a rare exception when there was a high-band level that didn't have subordinates. Bo had one of these positions and it afforded him not only the window cubicle (the low-band second levels had the credenza, but not the window) but also an additional $75 per month. One other advantage, one that Bo would have gladly surrendered the $75 to keep, was that he did not have to report to Jeremy Harris, but to the District Manager.

Harris was a short, balding man rapidly losing his battle to keep his 38-inch waist. Jeremy Harris was a legend in his own mind. Bo thought, as most who worked for and with him did, that he was a pompous, arrogant bully with a severe Napoleonic complex. When once accused of the Napoleonic complex, he responded, "Napoleon is one of my heroes!" and smiled proudly.

Harris, for an unknown reason, always wore corduroy pants. Therefore, anyone could hear him approaching. Bo could hear him coming from the other side of the floor. He quietly hoped that he would ignite from the rubbing, but it wasn't going to happen this morning.

"I'll need that report on the homicide before lunch," Harris barked. Bo smiled at the word homicide when it was clearly TV police talk and not what the company's investigators called it. In fact, deaths were so rare that it was not clear what they should be called, Bo thought.

"Why?" Bo asked.

"The DM asked me to follow up."

"Who?" Bo knew of no one in all the years he'd worked at the phone company that had ever referred to a District Manager as a "DM."

"You know, the District Manager."

"I talked with her this morning, and she didn't say anything about it," Bo lied.

"Well, uh... she wanted me to be informed since I'm the head of the Investigators."

"You're so full of shit, Harris," Bo purposely mispronounced his name, "The 'DM' didn't even talk to you. I have a call into her office, and she won't be in until after lunch." Harris had ignored both insults. "Incidentally, I have faxed the report to her already."

Harris smiled. Bo immediately regretted telling Harris this because he would get the clerk to fax a copy back to him.

"Well, I thought we could work on this together, Bozo." Bo wondered why fate had named this jerk Bill and himself Bozo. Harris was already walking away, realizing he could get the report elsewhere. Bo quietly prayed for corduroy igniting and burning the source of any future Harris.

The company's System Instructions were detailed instructions on what should be done in the event of any number of things. It advised the proper procedures for any natural disaster, such as an earthquake, fire, et cetera, for the schedule of approvals of expenses as well as detailing all reimbursable expenses, and for the handling of unique, as well as common, personnel matters, such as the death of an employee. The schedule of approvals was detailed and required a great number of approvals. One CEO, pre-divestiture, proudly said, "I go to bed every night knowing one person cannot do much harm to this company."

Bo was reviewing the various forms for the death of an employee. One of the forms was the K-15, which was needed for any accident. One of the questions was, "How could this accident be avoided?"

"Clearly, the answer," Bo thought, "is don't open terminals that explode." Often, the review of accidents did lead to revised safety procedures which were distributed throughout the Company. Filling out the forms for an accident, he noticed that he couldn't answer how this could be avoided in the future. It was the first time Bo thought that this might not be an isolated incident, but he wondered if there were several of these planted throughout the city. If this were true, it would literally stop all field telephone repairs. He would let Healy know his thinking.

Bo called Lt. John Healy but found that he was out and left a message. Bo also wanted to leave early so that he could pick up his son on time. He did not want to give Gloria anything to harp on. Bo decided that he would take blank forms and do the work over the weekend.

HOW'S YOUR MOTHER?

While Bo was picking up Jimmy, DeMarius Thomas was arriving at his apartment. He lived in one of the projects in South Central Los Angeles, but also had gotten an apartment out in the San Fernando Valley, where he lived what he fancied to be a double life like a James Bond agent.

DeMarius had developed a chameleon type of personality that had probably kept him alive. He could be whatever you wanted him to be. It was this trait that had really been the key in the anti-gang program. DeMarius had been the poster boy for the program. Councilman Arlington Johnson cried when DeMarius first shared his story of when he was six years old that he witnessed his mother's death. The tragic story of Anita Thomas had most of Los Angeles crying as they watched on the television.

It was a time when everyone needed something that provided hope in Los Angeles. The councilman could always use the good press, although most thought he would continue to get elected until he was dead or caught in corrupt dealings. Arlington had almost certainly participated in some excesses, but he was investigated only once, and he had set up the naïve reporter in an interview by feeding false information from his staff so that when all the facts came out, it appeared that he had been targeted for investigation solely because he was Black. No one dared risk the chance of being wrong on the slightest accusation with the esteemed councilman. He had become a hero in the community because he had beaten the oppression of the white man. The crowning statement from the police chief, who even white people considered a fascist, was that "where there is smoke, there is fire." The police chief had inadvertently given Councilman Johnson his eternal campaign slogan—"Yes, there is fire—fire in my heart to make this city better!"

Everyone watching DeMarius's teary-eyed tale believed Arlington Johnson was making the city better that day.

The President of the telephone company was at the news conference. He needed this good press since he had not had the best of public relations during his time as the company leader. The company, which in the business community could have been accused of not being that smart, but never accused of being dishonest, was reeling from annual scandals of overbilling for late payment, improper accounting of investments, and influencing the Public Utilities Commission. He had deftly placed blame on other individuals, but, finally, the board of directors had asked him who was running the operation anyhow. This had made him even less endeared to employees, a concept some would have guessed to be impossible.

When Bob Foster had become an officer of the company, he had hired an image consultant with his own money; he had a six-way mirror, watching himself when he got dressed and he had a fashion expert select his wardrobe for his slimmed-down body he'd acquired through the assistance of a personal trainer. Still, nature had cursed him with thick eyebrows and almost black eyes, the sort of brows that gave beauty to Brooke Shields, but which made Bob Foster look like a mean squirrel.

Foster created an atmosphere that was absolutely void of joy and stimulated fear even in top performers. The only joy that he aroused was in his wake. After a visit from him, he stimulated some of the best executive insults in modern times. They ranged from a story that he was the first successful charisma bypass surgery patient to the not-so-funny statement that he could single-handedly take care of the 5000-person downsizing by just talking individually with each employee. One of the retiring executives wrote in his resigning letter that "Life is too short to work for assholes."

But, at the news conference, Bob Foster was smiling, albeit a smile that looked painted on.

The irony was that although DeMarius had witnessed his mother's death, it had not been a story of a heroic mother desperately protecting her child as villains came and violated her and killed her. However, this is the story DeMarius told the television audience from the eyes of a terrified and tragic six-year-old peeking out at his helpless mother being attacked and killed by a group of unknown assailants, presumably gang members. Now DeMarius was trying to break from the environment that had killed his mother but had allowed him to exist until this "miracle of bright light" had given him "the only option he ever had in his life." This was the birth of the 'Bright Lights' program.

A sympathetic rookie police officer named Patricia Romner had asked DeMarius dozens of closed-ended questions, with DeMarius pointing and nodding or shaking his head until the essence of the story evolved. As Officer Romner related her story to the press, she noted with curiosity that she had experienced similar childhood trauma when she was a child. Patricia felt that God had placed her here to facilitate DeMarius telling his story in comparison to the eighteen years it had taken her to face her tragic experience.

DeMarius really didn't care what would happen to him as he killed his mother. He knew he would not miss her. She was barely present for him anyway. She had not been addicted to crack when she was pregnant with DeMarius. She only drank and did a little coke. She almost was abstinent for the last five months because her main source of income had been stopped by her distended stomach. The brothers didn't find her as attractive during her pregnancy. She had her tubes tied as DeMarius was born, so she wouldn't be plagued with another involuntary hiatus from sex and drugs.

It was somewhat of a minor miracle that DeMarius had been born without difficulty. He showed no physical ailments from an addicted mother. It was as if he was detached from her during the prenatal period. DeMarius clearly felt detached from her during the postnatal period. However, killing her was not an act of a necessarily abused boy striking back. If DeMarius, at age six, could have described it in modern psychobabble, he might have said he'd been neglected or maybe even abandoned, but not abused. DeMarius had seen others killed in the projects and saw that they were often considered heroes or, at least, elevated in status with their peers. He wanted to know if it was hard to do—to kill someone. DeMarius found out it wasn't very hard.

He had learned from his mother to "just give them what they want, and you get yours." DeMarius was giving policewoman Patricia Romner what she wanted when she led his story to the heroic mother tale; he was giving all of L.A. what they wanted with a hope of a gang alternative, he was giving Bob Foster his desperately needed good press, and he was giving Arlington Johnson easy re-election.

He was also giving Freddie his own access to the vital telecommunication network of Los Angeles. DeMarius had given Freddie something he needed from when they first met. DeMarius had moved to stay with his grandmother after his mother was killed. Freddie lived across the street with his own grandmother after his mother died from cancer. Freddie and DeMarius never knew the actual circumstances of the other's mother's deaths. As much as they could be friends and partners, neither trusted the other enough to share their experience.

DeMarius always got better deals as Freddie moved up the gang echelon. He wasn't afraid to do his fair share of killing because he liked it and was good at it. He liked to endear himself to the victim and then surprise them when he killed them. He would come back to Freddie and say, "I surprised them to death."

DeMarius was the perfect pick for the 'Bright Lights' pilot program. Freddie had arranged for some special tutoring to "reflect the telco culture." This only added to the arsenal of tools for DeMarius had become quite an accomplished actor.

DeMarius and Freddie were 27 now and had gotten to this age

by never trusting anyone. There were few males in their late twenties in South Central Los Angeles. Joining a gang often got one killed or jailed before making it to one's late twenties. Not joining a gang often got you killed just because you were such a standout and such an exception. Many others just got out. They moved to another geography, whether it be west to Inglewood, which may have been only marginally better, or completely out of the city. Very few could experience the longevity of gang membership that DeMarius and Freddie enjoyed.

Probably the major reason that they endured was that they were not only ruthless and prolific killers, but they were also clever killers. The real motive of the murder was slightly different from the truth, and often, the murderers themselves were manipulated or were killed by others who were manipulated. Often, a suggestion that some homeboy had "dissed" another would set off a chain of killings and revenge killings that often purged the gang of potential rivals. There seemed to be a never-ending supply of new potential members who felt special and honored to be asked by DeMarius and Freddie to belong to their gang.

It was the difference in the murder of Terry Simpson that had activated DeMarius's antenna. It was just the type of killing that Freddie would do. He felt a little hurt that Freddie might not trust him. In fact, he found it hard to believe, but he had to consider it a possibility because if it was and he ignored it, then he would certainly be dead within a month.

It did not seem to him that it was reasonable for Freddie to suspect him of anything. He had never considered it himself until he started living "the straight life." It was ironic that DeMarius felt comfortable with his life, although he never thought of it in those terms, but that he and Freddie had been together, and they would stay together. It was Freddie who'd thought of this 'Bright Lights' program because he could see that there was always a higher level of danger on the street. Freddie saw this as a way of increasing control on the street by "listening in" on the other gangs, suspected members of their gang, or the police. DeMarius saw that Freddie had seen this as a way to put another barrier between him and some dumb, doped-up punk on a drive-by. The surprise that neither Freddie nor DeMarius foresaw was that they had discovered a whole new market selling to telephone company employees.

It was this new market that DeMarius took a few extra dollars from. He could set any price he wanted because most of the telephone employees were relatively new, and their habits had either not become addictive, or had not yet outstripped their income or possessions. It was not the money that DeMarius wanted. It was the power and the new echelon of living. DeMarius could have almost any woman he wanted. He had come to like white women. Some wanted to be told stories of the gang. They were like groupies. They were proud to have made it with a gang banger. It excited them. He had seen too many brothers killed in their sleep. Black ladies did not tolerate the "dis" of anybody.

The respect that Freddie and DeMarius gave women had more than once saved their lives. Boastful wannabes would always tell their women that they were planning to move up in the gangs and either talk with their friends as if the women weren't even there or confide in a lover's whisper. Freddie and DeMarius would either take a preemptive strike, avoid any ambush and send others in their place, or arrange a "ricochet" murder.

The ricochet murder was a FreMar trademark. It was rather simple. You wanted party "A" dead, so you would kill party "B," whose death would be avenged and ensure that it was obvious that party "A" was known as the murderer.

In one case, it set off a chain of 16 retaliatory murders and still hadn't gotten the correct party. DeMarius finally called up party "A" and told him that he was aware that "they" were going to try to get him that night. DeMarius told "A" to stay at his place and trust no one until DeMarius himself could come over. He went over, and the guy asked him how he knew it was coming. DeMarius looked at him, smiled, and said, "Because 'they' is me, motherfucker. Surprise!" and shot him with nine hollow points.

The real seduction of this other life was not the women, however. It was the entree to a different kind of life. He attended Lakers games in the company chauffeur-driven cars and sat in company seats with various celebrities and the Vice President of Marketing. He sat with sports figures, movie stars, and politicians. He wanted to be with them, and they wanted to be with him. He had become a symbol of an improving Los Angeles. The company had rented him a tux, and he had gone to the Academy Awards. He had even been paid overtime since he was not management, and he had been "loaned" to Marketing for business meetings. The publicity of the 'Bright Lights' program had attracted other business leaders, and they wanted to know how they could participate. They also wanted to know what they were getting into. Nothing told them this better than one of the program participants. No participant told them better than DeMarius.

It became even better when the Vice President of Marketing, Tim Wallace, developed a liking for cocaine. It was the first time that DeMarius didn't tell something to Freddie. He told Freddie of the extra "marketing" activities but not of this additional distribution channel. It became quite significant because Tim not only bought to satisfy his own habit, but for several women and other executives in other companies. This gave DeMarius an unprecedented opportunity to "run" with the executive level of the phone company and executives of their business customers.

But it turned out that Freddie felt left behind. He still was dealing with the gang organization. He didn't have any celebrity fun. In fact, he felt that as long as he was still in the neighborhood, it was better to go as unnoticed as possible.

But he missed DeMarius. He also became jealous of the fun DeMarius seemed to be having. Where DeMarius still did not trust anyone, Freddie had begun to love and need DeMarius as a brother. The time in college, which wasn't marked by the constant vigilance required within the gang, had allowed a real bonding between them. Freddie felt that DeMarius may have been less committed to him than he was to DeMarius.

THIS MAKES NO SENSE

The next morning, Bo went over the documents he had gotten from the records he'd copied from Jenny's computer. One thing jumped out at him. The trouble report noted that the caller had requested a specific technician—DeMarius Thomas. Bo thought that this was a very rare request, but not impossible. In any event, he needed to follow up with Jenny. He had called her, and she was available at 9:30. He arrived at the garage and typed in the code that Jenny had given him.

Telephone installer and repair technicians' garages were remarkably the same throughout the entire United States. Most were built shortly after World War II. Surrounded by 10-foot wire fences with razor wire above it, were two to three buildings, and a significant parking lot that could accommodate all the telephone trucks as well as technician's personal vehicles.

There were some assigned parking spots for managers and visitors. Bo pulled into one of the visitor's slots. The buildings at this garage—and there were two—were a storage facility that had tools, paper cups and plates, office supplies and customer premise equipment (phones, wiring connectors, etc.). The other building had inside parking for about 30 telephone trucks as well as several offices, kitchen, and an assembly room for all-hands meetings.

Bo walked in the office building and, although he was 15 minutes early, found Jenny ready for him. She stood at her desk, which was in a large office accommodating 10 supervisor's desks. She stood, grabbed some notes, nodded with her head for him to follow her into another office. When she had closed the door, she reached to touch his wrist and said, "There are no secrets for anything said in that bullpen of an office. In here, we can talk. Before we talk about this, I wanted to thank you for the other night. You were kind and a gentleman. I don't see much of that very often. Would you like to come over to dinner next week?"

"No problem. Yes!" Bo responded. He was completely distracted from the touch and barely heard what she said.

"I looked again at the trouble report," she said, after she pulled back her hand, "and the request of a specific technician was not the only oddity of the report. The call had come in from a pay phone in South Central LA, not even in the Valley. This makes no sense."

Bo said out loud, "I need to get this John Healy right away. Can we speak with DeMarius?"

Jenny told Bo that DeMarius was dispatched in the field working trouble cases, but that they could find him. Bo called Healy but was only able to leave a message. "Let's go talk with DeMarius!"

Jenny called dispatch and got the address where DeMarius was assigned. She added, "He has just gotten the trouble ticket and we are less than two miles away, so we won't be chasing him."

The address was just south of Riverside Drive across the street from Notre Dame High School. Bo told Jenny, "The son of President Reagan lived in this neighborhood. When I was going to high school here, you could see a car with a Secret Service Agent at the top of this cul-de-sac. The protection wasn't that secret, but, thinking about it, that might have been on purpose."

Jenny and Bo saw the telephone truck and got out of the car. Jenny said, "DeMarius is one of the 'Bright Lights' hires."

"His name sounds familiar," Bo replied.

DeMarius was inside the customer's house, so they rang and asked him to come outside. They all walked over to his truck.

Jenny introduced Bo, "This is Bo Connecticut from Pacific Bell's Security office. He had some questions that you might be able to help with the explosion with Terry."

DeMarius frowned, "I don't know anything about that."

Bo said, "The trouble report had asked for you specifically. Why didn't you take the trouble?"

DeMarius' eyes widened, "The trouble report asked for me? Are you sure? That makes no sense."

"Why didn't you go?"

"I asked Terry to take the trouble so I could go to the Lakers game. I did not know that I had been asked for. Who asked for me? What exactly happened with Terry?"

Bo could tell that DeMarius had no idea about this trouble request and was now really concerned about his involvement.

Bo said, "We just needed to know if you knew anything about it. You're right—it makes no sense. I think it might have even been a typo or some confusion by the repair clerk. Sorry to bother you at all. I am just checking a box here."

When they got back in the car, Jenny asked, "You stopped that abruptly. Why?"

Bo answered, "He is very involved. A very rare request for a tech, a 'Bright Lights' person from South Central and a repair request from a payphone from South Central are not just coincidence. Healy will not be happy with me."

Surprisingly, Healy was not upset. "You didn't know about the call origin or 'Bright Lights' involvement until spur of the moment. How was DeMarius' reaction?"

"He wanted to know more, but I said that this makes no sense, I was just checking the boxes," Bo responded.

Healy asked, "Did he buy that?"

"No!" said Bo.

Healy said, "Thanks, Bo. Let me think about this. Please let me know if you find any other information." Healy stared at his phone saying, "This makes no sense." Then, he re-thought. "It makes some sense."

☦

DeMarius had called Freddie immediately after Bo and Jenny left.

"I just got questioned about the explosion of the technician out here in the Valley by Pacific Bell security. He told me that I had been requested specifically for that trouble ticket.

You know anything about this?"

Freddie said, "Why would they request you? That makes no sense." Freddie was particularly pleased with his initial response.

DeMarius was trying to see if he could surprise Freddie into saying something that might indicate that Freddie knew something about this. "Heck, he didn't even deny it," DeMarius thought.

Freddie asked "Who could know what we are doing within 'Bright Lights' that would do something like this?"

Again, DeMarius thought that Freddie was more concerned about the program than being accused of anything. He answered, "I don't know."

Freddie said, "Who was the Security guy? Did he look like he was going to pursue this?"

DeMarius had to think—"First name was Bo. Last name was a state like Tennessee or something. And he gave me the checking-the-box dance and shut me down quickly. Yes, absolutely, he was going after this like a bulldog."

"Let me get back to you. You all right?" Freddie asked.

"I was a little shook, but I'm OK."

DeMarius looked at his phone thinking, "This makes no sense." He thought maybe Freddie wasn't involved in this.

Freddie had all the names and phone numbers of 'Bright Lights' members of the gang. He remembered that one of them worked as a clerk in the Security office. There were only a few females on the list, but he thought he would remember the name when he saw it. It was the third female's name on the list—Claire Turner. He wasn't able to recall her face, but he needed to call her anyway and knew she would remember his name and face.

When Claire answered the phone, she heard, "This is Freddie

Kane. How are you doing, Claire?"

She was momentarily shocked into silence. She also quickly realized that this was not a good thing for her. She meekly responded, "I'm okay."

"That's good news, Claire. I need a favor if you can help me out. There is a security guy named Bo. His last name may be a state like Tennessee or something like that. Do you know him?" he asked.

"Yes, Bo Connecticut."

"Claire, I need his home address."

Claire was exceptionally nervous because this would be something she would never give out normally, but the repeated use of her name—"Claire"—suggested that Freddie expected an answer and certainly implied a threat. She knew damn well if she didn't do this favor, there would be consequences.

She said, "I will have to call you back." She was not sure exactly where to find this or even if she could find it. In addition, she needed time to think.

Freddie responded quickly in a much less friendly tone. "Claire, I need this in the next 10 minutes. You have my number on caller ID. Do not let me down." Then he hung up.

Claire left her desk and headed straight for the women's restroom, where she promptly threw up.

Bo dropped off Jenny at the garage. He was already in the Valley and had been invited to a family dinner to celebrate Jimmy making the soccer all-star team. Jimmy had phoned Bo. "Robert, who is at my school, made the team too. He said you know his dad, who is a policeman."

"What's his last name?" Bo asked.

"Healy. Robert Healy!" Jimmy said excitedly. "And he is coming to dinner tonight. By the way, Grandma is picking us up at school and bringing us to dinner. Her yard is much better for playing soccer—and Mom knows and it is okay with her."

"I do know him. Look, Jimmy, I'm a little busy now. Congrats Mr. All-Star. See you tonight!"

Bo was going to work from his apartment over the garage on the Chandler Estates. The apartment had a kitchenette with a small refrigerator and stove. It had one bedroom with a shower. There was a small table for eating. The den housed a TV, a couch that had a roll-out bed used when Jimmy stayed and his desk and bookcases. The desk had a window that viewed the back yard's beautiful English-style garden. The garden reminded him of his mom's garden and love for it.

Approximately two miles east of Van Nuys Blvd, where Chandler Blvd (where the area got its name) just merged on to Van Nuys in a wide curve, there were several full acre-sized lots that had custom-built homes that had a large and beautiful grass and tree parkway separating a pair of two-lane one way streets going east and west. Most of the homes had fences and/or landscaping providing privacy and security.

A retired actor friend of Duncan's had made this available to Bo after they sold the house. It was a sweetheart deal where he paid utilities for the property, which never exceeded $400. He had gone through the Chick-fil-A drive thru and gotten the regular chicken sandwich and waffle fries for his lunch.

First order of business, Bo updated his boss on the new developments in the Terry Simpson case. She indicated she was now getting inquiries directly from the President's office. Bo told her he would keep her up to date.

Bo suddenly felt exhausted and decided to take a short nap.

THE COVERUP IS WORSE THAN THE CRIME

Betty Fernandez had worked in the office of the President at Pacific Bell through three different Presidents. She liked two of them—the current one, not so much. Her job description read a lot like a Chief of Staff. The title was Director of Strategic projects. 'Bright Lights' had fallen to her to monitor and ensure success, which the current President defined as "only good news." Betty, who graduated from UC Berkeley and then got her MBA from Stanford, had been part of Management New Hire program, where she was provided with several assignments in the first five years, but was promoted to second level management after the first eighteen months due to excellent performance reviews from both bosses and peers. She had been handpicked by the President six years ago for this job that included her promotion to Director. She remained in this role now working with the current President, Bob Foster. Foster had replaced almost everyone on the executive staff, but she still survived.

Betty was annoyed that Foster always treated her as a personal lackey. The job had been a fountain of learning under the previous regimes, but had become increasingly annoying as time went on. Foster liked to blame the messenger on any bad news.

The update on the employee death had just turned into a possible "bad news situation" because of the suggestion of the involvement of DeMarius Thomas, who had been the face of the program when it was introduced. Betty wasn't sure what Bob Foster would do with this information, but she knew he would want to know ASAP. She went to his office and asked the secretary, "Is Bob in today?"

The secretary, Irene Darling, who only answered phones, welcomed any visitors and managed Bob's calendar, had obviously been selected for her beauty and charm. It was hard not to like her, but she didn't type or have any duties other than being basically a hostess.

"He actually is, but has someone with him now. I believe they should be done in five or so minutes, then I could get you in. Would you like some coffee?" Irene answered.

"No thanks, Irene. Thank you." Betty did marvel at how Irene could be so pleasant while working so closely with Foster.

Foster walked out with his guest, saying, "Irene, will you please guide Mr. Jenkins out through our maze to the front lobby?" Turning to Jenkins, "Bill, you are a very important customer of ours. I will ensure that your move has no glitches with your telephone and data services."

Jenkins said, "Thanks a lot, Bob."

After they left the office, Foster saw Betty. "You want to talk with me?"

Betty said, "Yes, it's about 'Bright Lights.'"

He turned and walked toward his office, saying, "Come in."

"That guy is a member of the board at my country club. He caught me at golf on Saturday and asked to see me today. What a waste of time, but he can help me with any club issues, so I made time. What about 'Bright Lights'?"

Betty, silently in her mind, said, "Thank you for asking, Bob. I am fine." But, out loud said, "The installer killed in the explosion may have been aimed for DeMarius Thomas, who is the face…"

Foster interrupted, "I know who he is. How is he involved?"

"He had been requested as the repair tech in the initial call."

"That makes no sense. I have never heard of that."

"Exactly!" Betty responded. "And the call for the trouble case in the San Fernando Valley came from a pay phone in South Central. Our security investigator has discovered this."

"Is the investigator competent?" Foster asked.

"I am told he is the best we have."

"Then, as of now, I want you personally to take over the investigation. Have him removed from the investigation. Get any and all paperwork sent to you immediately."

Betty stood quietly, then asked, "Why?"

Foster shouted, "Because I cannot have any issues right now with 'Bright Lights!'" He seemed to catch himself and then said, "This is the death of one of our employees and I want to personally be involved in every aspect of it."

"Bullshit!" Betty thought, but said, "I will get right on it."

Foster, without saying anything more, looked down at his desk and shooed her out with his hand. "Close the door, will you?"

Betty called Carol Dellamor, Bo's boss, who had just given her the update this morning. They had been in the same Management Hire program together and had been equally successful in their careers. They were more friends than rivals, but the different geographies of Betty living in Northern California and Carol living in Southern California didn't really nourish their friendship. Betty was wrestling at telling the complete truth of the President's demand or just part of it. Betty decided she would reach out directly to Bo Connecticut.

At the same time, Bob Foster had called the city councilman of Los Angeles, Arlington Johnson. Arlington said he would reach out to the Police Chief, who owed Arlington a favor because of continued budgetary support. Within a half hour, John Healy was told that the case was not his anymore. It would be handled by the Chief of Police staff.

At the Pacific Bell security office, Jeremy Harris, walking with his signature corduroy pants making a rubbing noise because his thighs were so big, entered the office of Carol Dellamor. Claire Turner was so focused that she didn't even hear him.

"What are you doing here?" Jeremy asked.

Claire screeched, "You scared me!" She had turned around and Jeremy saw she was crying. Without even thinking of lying, she blurted, "Freddie wants Bo's home address and I have ten minutes to give it to him."

Jeremy Harris always wanted to be liked in the office but had no idea how to get this done. He admired Claire for leaving a terrible life to be in South Central and he admired Bo because he was so good at the job. But he always tried to be the "big shot", thinking that would get him the respect and friendship he wanted. It never did.

"Claire, please just sit down for a second." Jeremy said, surprising himself with his own concerned tone. "You know we can't give personal information to outsiders."

She looked at him almost whispering, "You don't understand. This is not a request. Freddie will not just kill me, but also my whole family. He has done it before. I cannot say 'NO' to him. I found this 3x5 card in Carol's files. It has the address of 14826 Weddington Street in Van Nuys with 14826 crossed out and 14806 replacing it."

Jeremy knew that he should report this to the police, but also knew that missing the time limit from Freddie threatened Claire and her family's lives. He knew it might not be immediately, but knew it would be eventually.

"Call him and give him the 14826 address." Jeremy said. "It looks like it is an old address and you could defend your actions if it came up eventually. I will call Bo and let him know what is going on and he can take any action he wants to."

WEDDINGTON STREET

Winifred "Win" Connecticut looked at the clock and saw she had an hour before she needed to pick up Jimmy and his friend. She was enjoying that she could again be trusted with having Jimmy with her. Gloria had been furious about Win leaving Jimmy sleeping in the car while she was "watching" him. Although nothing had happened, Win knew she was wrong for letting it happen and regretted it.

While working in her garden, she was reflecting on her life. She had married young and was pregnant right away, but had a miscarriage at six weeks. Her husband, Theodore "Ted" Connecticut had been a house painter. They both were so young that they didn't even quite understand the loss. Both had been orphaned at early ages. They both had left their foster homes at age 18 and began working immediately. They met at the hardware store where she was a bookkeeper, and he was in the warehouse.

When she got pregnant the second time, they were both

thrilled. They celebrated with champagne. She had rarely ever drank, but this was special. Four months later, Ted fell from a ladder at the warehouse, hit his head and died. The warehouse company tried to blame Ted, but Win's friend, Mary Alice Kaufmann, had a father who was a lawyer, who secured $10,000 in damages from the company for Win. Ted had also gotten a life insurance policy for $50,000 that Win was unaware of. She entered a period of depression and began drinking more, but soon stopped because she was afraid of injuring the baby. The insurance and lawsuit money had let her buy the house on Weddington Street, which she loved. It was a peaceful neighborhood and the house was only five years old when she bought it. She was able to pay cash and never had a house payment.

When the baby was born, her only visitor was Mary Alice, but a nurse had befriended her as well. Win remembered that this nurse introduced her to Scotch as they celebrated the baby's birth. She also suggested the name "Bozo". Win had subsequently wished for a "mulligan" on that, but Bo was a really cool name for her wonderful son.

Mary Alice's dad, William Kaufmann, was a lawyer at JPL (Jet Propulsion Labs) and had gotten her a secretary job there when she could work. William and Mary Alice were Bo's godparents. Win was remembering how grateful she was to the Kaufmann family. William had passed some ten years ago, but Mary Alice remained a great friend. In fact, she and Duncan were her only friends outside of AA (Alcoholics Anonymous). Mary Alice had driven her to her first meeting.

Win had worked for JPL for over 30 years and she loved the

work, the company and the people she worked with. When Bo was in high school, she had gotten sick and saw a doctor at UCLA who told her that she had stage 4 cancer and "should get her affairs in order." Her health had become a problem at home and was beginning to be a problem for work. Mary Alice had stepped in and took her to a Doctor at USC. This doctor had put her on an experimental chemo program, which had worked for her. She became cancer-free. Four years later, the cancer returned, but the chemo had done its job again. JPL had a policy of "keeping your job open" for six months when you had a long-term illness. However, JPL had switched her job at six months so they could extend "keeping her job open" until she could finally return. She had asked her boss how he could violate policy like that. He had said, "Win, I have learned that all companies could do anything they want if they want to do it. And, for you, we wanted to do it."

Win had never really had a man in her life. She dated and had friends, but no one had really appealed to her as a life partner. She also felt that Bo needed her because he had no father. She was asked by Mary Alice, "Haven't you met anyone at your AA meetings?"

She answered, "Mary Alice, I was told early on that 'the odds are good, but the goods are odd.'"

Duncan Barrett had come to an AA meeting for some research for one of his movie roles. They had gone to coffee and continued to see each other to this day. Win felt they both loved each other, but neither had ever brought up marriage. She was looking forward to seeing Duncan tonight.

As she looked at her watch, she needed to go get Jimmy. She would bring them back to play until dinner.

JACK MCGUIGAN

☦

When Bo woke up, he saw he had ten messages. One from his boss, Carol; one from a 415 area code; one from John Healy; six from Jeremy Harris and one from Arlington Johnson. He called Carol first—the message was: "The Terry Simpson case is no longer our case. It will be handled by Betty Fernandez on the President's staff. She may be calling you."

Bo called John Healy back next. John answered saying, "This case has been taken away from me."

Bo said, "Really? I was told the same thing."

Healy said, "I don't like this. It doesn't feel right."

Bo said, "It feels like someone or lots of someone's want to control the narrative."

Healy said, "Or cover it up."

Bo said, "Hey, I heard your son is an all-star. So is mine. He is coming to dinner tonight at my wife's house to celebrate. You want to come? We could think on this and discuss it some more." Bo gave Healy the address and the time.

Bo listened to the messages from Harris. He said, "911", "This is urgent", "Please call", "What is your address?"

Bo stopped listening and called Harris's number.

Harris answered right away. "Oh, Bo! Great."

"What's the problem?"

"Claire, our clerk, you know, is part of the 'Bright Lights' program. She got a call from Freddie Kane this morning asking for your home address. He gave her 30 minutes to get this. Claire says he is a stone cold killer and if he doesn't get it, he would not only kill her but her whole family."

"What did you guys do?"

"We had found a 3x5 card that had two addresses—14826 Weddington, which was crossed out and 14806 was put in. We gave him the 14826 address. Bo, I didn't tell the police or anyone else because I wanted to let you know first."

"Jeremy, thank you. And thank you for calling me like a banshee. I'll take care of this. Tell Claire to tell no one about this."

Bo called Healy back immediately. He explained about the call from Freddie. "My mom lives at 14806 Weddington AND has your son and my son at her house after she picks them up at school. I am five minutes away and I am going there now."

John Healy replied, "You know, Bo, you are the target here. I will be there shortly. Make sure you don't get yourself shot."

Both got off the phone and went to their cars. Bo called his mom's phone but was only able to leave a message.

†

Dr. Dredd and Tracer had been called by Freddie and told to put a scare into the house at 14826 Weddington Street. No one needed to get killed, but it didn't matter to Freddie. They were told to get it done this afternoon. They got there about 3:00 pm. As was their usual plan, they drove past the target house twice about 10 minutes apart. They parked on Bevis Avenue, which dead ended on Weddington, so they could go left or right. In fact, if they drove straight, they would drive right into a 20-foot white birch tree.

The parking spot gave them a great view of the house.

Tracer said, "I don't want to kill anyone. It would, for sure, come back on us."

"Absolutely, my man. Don't use the machine gun, just your Glock and put 3 rounds higher than six feet."

Dr. Dredd replied, "Let's get it done."

The plan was to turn left on Weddington, take the shots and leave in a hurry. They stopped at the stop sign just before the turn and saw an old Taurus driving fast and pull in front of the house four doors down. They saw a man throw the door open and run to the house.

Tracer said, "This doesn't feel right. Let's boogie."

Dr. Dredd turned right and was almost hit by a car coming off Kester Avenue. The two gang members saw a large Black man driving fast, but not so fast that he didn't stare at them. Dredd floored it and turned right on Kester.

Healy saw the guys as he turned but was more concerned about his son and Bo. He saw the Taurus up the street and parked nose to nose and got out. He ran to the front yelling Bo's name. "Nobody's here. They must be returning from school."

Just then, Win pulled in her driveway. Both boys hopped out of the car simultaneously yelling, "Hi, Dad!" then they both looked at each other and laughed. Both Bo and Healy quickly and surreptitiously holstered their guns. Both boys didn't notice. Win did.

"Both you boys go in the back and practice your kicking," Win yelled.

She then looked at Bo and John Healy saying, "Both YOU boys come in for coffee!"

She walked into the house then the kitchen and pulled out Dunkin' K-cups for the Keurig. "Sit down," she said, and she pointed to the corner booth. She pulled her chair away so both had to sit in the booth. Bo felt the familiar setting where he was interrogated as he was growing up. He was sure Healy was not going to enjoy this. John Healy looked at Win and felt her authority. She was barely 5'2", and still slender with a whisper of gray hair at each temple surrounded by dark red hair. She had that presence that most cops had and the eyes that looked at you and already knew the answer to all the questions they were going to ask.

"What's your name, young man?"

"John Healy, ma'am."

"And why are you at my house brandishing weapons?" Bo remembered his mother never had been subtle.

Bo answered saying, "John is a detective I have been working with on a case."

She asked, "The technician explosion case?"

Bo had never talked to her about any of his cases and hadn't even seen her since this started.

"Okay, Bozo," Win said, using a name she only used when she was angry. "Do you think it takes a Phi Beta Kappa to figure out you would be involved in a telephone death that was on the front page?"

Healy offered, "We really can't talk about this now."

Win said, "How do you want your coffee, John?"

"Do you have cream and sugar?"

"Will half and half do?"

"Yes, ma'am. Thank you."

"John," she said as she put his coffee in front of him, "was your son in danger today?"

Healy's shoulders slumped as he realized that was exactly what happened.

"Yes, I think so."

He looked at Bo, saying, "Since we are off this case, this is no longer an ongoing investigation."

Bo smiled, "Just so you know, I have never lasted that long at this table when she is questioning me."

Bo and John outlined the turn of events in the last three days. Win listened and nodded without interrupting or asking a question. When they finished, John Healy said, "I forgot in all the rushing. I saw two obvious gangbangers leaving the neighborhood as I drove in. I saw your Taurus here, so I came here."

"Damn, speaking of forgetting, I had been called by my office that Freddie had asked for my home address. What I didn't tell you, John, was that they gave them 14826 Weddington."

"So?" asked John.

"I used to live at 14826. This house is 14806. It has been my mom's house for over 30 years. I grew up here. When Gloria and I got married, 14826 was our first house. When we separated, I put 14806 for mailing my pay stub. I saw my mom often enough to pick it up and my current residence didn't lend itself to easy mail pickup."

"They found an old 3x5 card that I had scribbled out the old address and put this one. They were afraid of Freddie and not giving them something, so they gave him the old address."

Win said, "So, gentlemen, what's next? It seems that the powers that be are interested in protecting the 'Bright Lights' program."

Bo said, "Mom, would you mind staying at Duncan's at least for tonight. You know he wouldn't mind."

"I think that's a good idea, Ms. Connecticut," Healy added.

"Call me Win, please. Yes, I'll go. And what are you two going to do?"

"I don't know. John, can you join us at dinner tonight? We can talk later," Bo said.

"I will answer both questions. Win, Bo and I are no longer off the case. And, Bo, when is dinner?" John asked.

Simultaneously, Bo and Win said, "Let's go now!"

FAMILY DINNER

As far back as Bo could remember, Sunday dinner was family dinner. Often, it was just his mother and him. Even in her drinking times, it was a constant. It could have visitors and people that were friends, but family was the main invitee. The definition of family expanded and contracted over the years. Bo remembered Mary Alice, her friend, and Mary Alice's father, who got her the job at JPL, were frequent attendees until the father passed away.

There was the "AA Birthday", which featured an epic food fight. Remarkably, everyone helped clean up—all saying they were "cleaning up the wreckage of their past." Evidently, an often repeated saying in AA.

And the Sunday dinner did not have to occur on Sunday. The "dinner" could be for birthdays, celebrations of any sort, major announcements (Gloria saying she was pregnant with Jimmy, Bo and Gloria and Bo announcing their separation), or for no good reason at all. Bo thought, "Like tonight." But he was wrong.

The seating for any event or meeting usually follows a pattern of people sitting in "their seat." At work, the boss most often sits at the head of the table and people gravitate to the seat they usually sit in.

The normal seating had Duncan at the head of the table (it was his house). Win sat to his right, Gloria to his left with Jimmy next to her. Bo sat next to Jimmy. Bill Martini sat next to Win.

If the dinner was at Win's house, Win and Duncan changed seat positions.

Tonight, the dinner was at Duncan's. The boys sat at the end of the table totally talking about their soccer games. Bill sat next to Gloria and Win was sitting at the head with Duncan on her right. Bo was sitting between Duncan and John Healy.

Bo almost asked why Win was sitting at the head of the table, but was stopped as Win asked John, "Tell us about yourself, John." John looked at Bo. Bo responded with a look that was not going to rescue him.

"I am a policeman, Win, as you know."

Bo added, "He is actually a police Lieutenant in homicide."

John continued, "I have been with the force for fourteen years. Always with LAPD. Duncan, I've actually seen you a couple of times. Once, you were a speaker at my academy graduation dinner. And we were both at the retirement of Tom Bradley before he became mayor."

Duncan said, "Tom was really good at both jobs during difficult times."

Bo asked, "Does your wife take Brian to practice? I have seen her there."

"No," John said, "that's my sister. My wife, Brian's Mom, was killed in a car crash when Brian was 5 years old. My sister, Lorraine, has helped ever since. She was married to this world-class joke and was separated while the divorce went through at the same time. So, it worked out. And it continues to work out. She is a blessing and Brian and I adore her."

That ended the interrogation of John. The rest of the discussion was about the food. As we finished the meal, Win suggested that the boys go off and kick the ball around. They hopped up immediately as Win yelled, "We'll call you for dessert."

"Now I have something I want to discuss."

Bo thought that she was going to be discussing the afternoon's events and said, "I don't think this is appropriate at this time."

Win countered, "I don't think you would ever think this topic is appropriate. Bo, have you had sex since you and Gloria separated?"

"WHAT?!" Bo said.

"Answer me."

Bo looked around and most were as shocked as him, except Duncan was smiling.

"No, but I don't think that is anybody's business."

Win turned to Gloria. "Gloria, have you had sex since you two separated?"

"I don't have to answer that!"

Win continued, "Bill, have you and Gloria had sex?"

Bill held up his hands saying, "Absolutely not!!"

Gloria stared menacingly at Win, saying, "And neither have I," almost in a slow whisper but clearly audible to all.

"Then why aren't you divorced?"

Bo answered, "You know it's for the insurance."

"Is that it? The only reason? Is there a chance you guys will get back together?"

A simultaneous "NO" from both Bo and Gloria.

Duncan, still smiling, said, "Then I would like to pay for the insurance for Gloria and Jimmy. They have been staying here for almost 3 years and I consider them part of my family. Bo, you have stepped up to be a father and a pretty good ex-husband, but you both need to move on with your lives."

Bo looked at John, who was now also smiling. Bo asked, "Why did you ask Bill that question?"

Win answered, "Because any fool except you three see that there is no life in the marriage and there is an obvious attraction between Gloria and Bill."

Gloria asked, "How do you know this?"

"Because nobody likes to help with the dishes like Bill does."

Bo turned to Bill and asked, "Is this what you wanted to talk about?"

"Yes, but I wouldn't have done this way," he said, as he held out his hands palms up.

Duncan said, "I asked Bill about this in a circuitous way and Bill said he would not do anything that would injure his friendship with you, Bo. And, for one, I couldn't watch this anymore."

Win said, "And me either, why do you think I am doing this now?"

John said, "This is a really interesting dinner." Everyone laughed except Bo.

"What will Jimmy think?" Bo asked.

Win called, "Hey Jimmy, hey Brian, come back for dessert.

The boys ran back and were winded and sweaty.

Win said, "Jimmy, your folks are finally going to get divorced. What do you think?"

"Finally! Where's dessert?"

"Jimmy, your Mom and Bill may start dating."

"What a surprise—NOT!! Bill is already part of the family and I love him. Dad, are you okay with this?"

Bo looked around. Everybody was smiling. "That's not the question, Jimmy. The question is… Where's the dessert?"

Duncan said, "You boys go to the freezer. There are ice cream sandwiches for everybody."

Bo actually felt relieved. It had been a burden of "still married" and not married. Gloria had to feel the same way. He was not certain that his emotions had any more juice after this afternoon and evening. But he loved ice cream sandwiches and began to smile.

Even the dogs Gladys and Knight seemed to smile.

WHAT'S NEXT?

After dessert, the boys went back to playing soccer. Bill went with Gloria to clean up the kitchen and dinner table—and Win joined them. Bo noticed that Win and Gloria walked away from the table with their arms interlocked. Bo thought that miracles never ceased.

Bo and John went into the den.

"What do you think we should do next?" John asked. Bo was almost surprised that John was asking him. Before he could answer, Gladys and Knight entered the room and Duncan stood in the doorway. Knight came over to Bo and affectionately wiped her drool on Bo's jeans. Gladys sat at John's feet and stared at him.

Duncan said, "Win told me about this afternoon—and everything else. I'm sure you're planning your next steps."

John looked at Bo, then said, "Look, Duncan, we don't know what we are going to do, but I, for one, want to keep the discussion to as few as possible. It was our sons who were in danger today and we have any possible official position or authority taken away from us, even research information within the organization." Bo remained quiet.

Duncan replied, "I can understand your thinking." Then much louder than Bo had ever heard Duncan speak, "the next time that I don't consider Bo and his family—AND HIS SON—part of my family…" He paused looking at Bo and John… "will be the first time. Additionally, it is exactly your removal from working directly with this case where I can help. I consider my contacts in the LAPD friends and they consider me a friend as well. I have gotten information in the past that should never have been shared. One more thing, no one will see me coming."

Bo turned to John and said, "John, Duncan has been able to keep counsel for all the time I have known him. He has also been a voice of reason in guiding me in my own personal decision making. And we don't know what we are going to do. We could use some thinking outside of ourselves here." Gladys barked once while still staring at John.

John raised his eyebrows a full inch. "I'm not going to argue with either of you—or the dogs."

Bo reached for his phone as it buzzed again. He had a number of missed calls and multiple messages. "Hey guys, I have calls and messages from three people that may have something to do with this. The calls are from Jeremy Harris, the one who alerted me about this afternoon… Another from Betty Fernandez, who works for the President. She is the one taking the case over from me. And one from Arlington Johnson, an LA City Council Representative. Since there are five from Jeremy, I'll play it first. I'll put it on speaker."

Bo, are you OK? I took Claire to my place. She called her home and her mom and sister are going to visit and stay with her aunt in Chula Vista for a while. I told Carol I was taking Claire home to her house because she felt too sick to drive. It was a phone message as Carol is out of the office. I have told no one else any of this. Please call me.
  Bo, please call.
  Bo, call dammit.
  Bo, call.

"I think I can guess the next one. Let me call him," Bo said. Duncan said "Beer?"

Bo and John nodded. John said, "Let me come with you."

As they walked down the hall, John continued, "Duncan, I didn't mean to be disrespectful."

Duncan interrupted, "I would have said the same thing if I was in your shoes. You don't know me. I want to help and I think I can."

John answered, "This could get very dangerous and I don't want anyone else to get hurt."

Duncan turned and stopped, "I promise I won't get into that level. Now, I think we need more than one beer. I am getting a six-pack."

"Good idea!" John replied.

Bo thanked Jeremy again. He felt a little ashamed after Jeremy explained that he was just trying to be a friend to Bo and was acting like a big shot all the time, which he now realized was stupid.

Jeremy said, "I am not very good at communicating with people sometimes." Bo had told Jeremy that his communication had been world-class.

When John and Duncan returned, Bo told them about the Jeremy phone call and that Claire and her family were now safe. "This next one is from Betty Fernandez, who has been told to take the case from me. My boss left an earlier message saying she would be calling me."

> *Bo, my name is Betty Fernandez. I am a Director of Special Projects and work directly for Bob Foster. He has asked me to take the Terry Simpson case over from you. I need to talk with you as soon as possible. I am a good friend of Carol Dellamor, who said you were competent, smart and an all-around good guy. I also spoke with Kate Fischer, who echoed the sentiment. That being said, I am not sure I could find two people who say the same thing about Bob Foster. But I need to look like I am doing what he asked. Please call me and then delete this message. Since I consider this a 'Mission Impossible,' I needed to say that."*

Bo deleted the message and went to Arlington Johnson's message.

> *Bo, I hope you remember me. We discussed one of your technicians a while back. I got a call from your President on an issue that touches the 'Bright Lights' program. I did call the Police Chief about it, but I have reconsidered that*

action and wanted your thoughts. Please call me when you get a chance.

"Well, we know now why you were removed from the case, John." Bo said.

Duncan said, "Is the explosion with the technician the start of all this?"

Both John and Bo simultaneously replied "Yes."

"Then is it worthwhile to review what we know about that? And do you have, pardon the jargon, a 'hunch' about what this means?"

John detailed all the critical elements of the crime scene. He also reviewed the pieces of information from Bo about the dispatch and repair process.

Bo hit the table hard saying "Damn! Yesterday, I talked with Jenny to get more detail about that. The repair ticket was weird in two ways. One, there was no problem with the telephone number. Two, the caller asked for a specific technician. We then went to the technician, DeMarius Thomas, and asked him about it. He was scheduled to work then, but got a chance to go to a Lakers game and asked Terry if he would take the case. The more we asked about it, the more distant and vague his answers became. Jenny, the supervisor at the garage, agreed with me."

John asked, "Is she the supervisor who was at the crime scene?"

Bo said, "Yes."

"Could she be in danger as well?"

"Shit, absolutely!"

Bo got his phone in his hand and dialed her number looking at his watch seeing 9:40 pm. It was answered on the fourth ring,

"Hello."

Bo almost yelled, "Jenny?"

"No. This is her mom."

"Mrs. Lee, this is Bo Connecticut. I work with Jenny. Is she around?"

"Yes, I'll get her. And thanks, Bo, for being so kind to her the other night."

It took two minutes. Jenny said, "Hi."

Bo started, "Jenny, I am sorry to call so late, but this is urgent. Do you have a place where you can go for a couple of days with your son and your mom?"

"You're scaring me, Bo."

"I received a threat to my son and my mom after we talked with DeMarius. We believe they got the wrong address, but we think a gang member came by their house, but the wrong house. I was advised this afternoon and only just realized that this could have been stimulated by our discussion with DeMarius."

Duncan mouthed, "We've got room here."

Bo continued, "For tonight, I have my son and ex-wife and mom at a place here in Studio City. Could you please pack a few things and come over here now? Please trust me that I think this is both urgent and necessary."

Jenny was quiet for a few seconds, "What is the address?"

After he gave it to her, Jenny said, "We'll be there by 11:00."

The five-bedroom house had never been as full as tonight. The cottage in the back held Jenny and the three boys. Jenny's son, Mark, brought his computer and played video games to the level that Jimmy and Robert termed "world-class." They talked and played games until 3:00 am. Duncan surrendered the master bedroom to Jenny and her mother. Duncan and Win shared another. Bo, John and Bill had the other rooms.

Jenny asked Bo to take a walk with her after introductions and the rationale of "abundance of caution" was given in the event of another explosion. The group was advised that other people were doing the same thing.

They walked a block in silence before Jenny looked at him saying "Abundance of caution? Bullshit!"

"Look, I realized that there might be real danger for you two seconds before I called. I know my address was compromised, but I don't think yours was, but I couldn't risk it," Bo said.

"Why is this happening?" she asked.

"I don't know, but here is what I think it is. I believe that DeMarius was the target of the explosion."

"You know I agree with that."

"But I think DeMarius called someone back at the gang. They, either with or without DeMarius's knowledge, wanted to derail the investigation. This afternoon, I was taken off the investigation at the phone company, and so was John by LAPD."

"Is this a big conspiracy? Would the company, the police and an inner city gang all work together on this?" Jenny asked.

"There must be different agendas at work here," Bo answered. "I also got a call from a city councilman this afternoon. He was called by Bob Foster and reached out to the Police Chief about the 'Bright Lights' program."

Jenny then turned and hugged Bo. She said, "I am really afraid here."

He hugged her back, and kissed the top of her head, saying, "Me, too."

THE ENEMY OF MY ENEMY IS MY FRIEND

After Bo called Jenny, he had forgotten about the phone calls from Betty Fernandez and Arlington Johnson. Arlington wanted to meet face-to-face and NOT near his house. Bo suggested Dupar's in Woodland Hills. Bo asked if John Healy could come with Bo. When Bo said he was a policeman, Arlington said, "That would be a good idea."

They decided to meet at 10:30. Arlington was concerned that someone would recognize him. He wanted to meet away from his district. When he showed up wearing a Dodgers cap, Levis, a semi-dirty sweatshirt and Converse high tops, even Bo didn't recognize him.

Arlington said, "I'm sorry about the long drive and my outfit. More and more, there are photographers taking pictures of semi-celebrities. Thus, the location and the outfit. I dragged the sweatshirt through the dirt and dusted it off. I had to hide it when I was leaving the house. My mother would never have let me leave with it on. As it was, I got a very judgmental 'Mom' look from her."

"The paparazzi," John said.

"Yes, and you must be John Healy. I am sorry, but I think you got moved off of a case because of me."

John raised his eyebrows, "I was taken off a case, but you…?"

Arlington looked first at John and then to Bo. "Bo," then a long pause, "I hope you remember our meeting at my office some time back?"

"Of course, Councilman!"

"Please call me 'Ar'—both of you. I felt a trust with you then and want to speak with you both without worrying about hearing any of this back or reading it in the newspaper."

Both Bo and John nodded saying, "Sure."

"Okay. As you may know, I was a proponent of the 'Bright Lights' program. Until recently, I even thought it was my idea. I met with both Freddie Kane and DeMarius Thomas because of a call from them. I had suggested paying the gangs to help stop graffiti. It was not well received from the police, the city administration, or the gangs. But they suggested getting some real jobs with the telephone company and other companies to offer something better than a gang and better than a fast-food job."

Arlington paused as he sipped his coffee.

He continued, "It was a little bit weird. It was on a block where I had received some complaints about residents having to cover all the front windows in their houses. When I followed up, the people said there was no problem. Later, I heard from others that Freddie didn't allow anyone to have front view access or cameras on the block—"for their own good." There was even a story that a family cat had been cut open and left in the back yard for someone who had not fully complied. In addition, I was told to park on another block and walk up." He gave a crooked smile and said, "I complied!"

The waitress came up and asked if we wanted anything besides coffee.

Bo said, "They have the best chocolate donuts. You need a knife and fork to eat one."

John said, "I'll have one."

Arlington said, "Me, too."

Bo said, "Me three."

The waitress smiled and left.

John said, "Wow! And not about the donuts," watching the waitress walk away.

Bo said, "Wait until you have the donuts."

All three laughed, despite the story.

Arlington relaxed. "The meeting was at his house, which was well kept. The lawn and landscaping were neat, but not remarkable. Same with the house. The paint was in good order, the roof was in good shape, but nothing said, "gang leader" or "drug dealer." But in the meeting, there was no doubt."

The donuts arrived. John took a bite and said, "Okay, WOW!" turning to Bo.

After the waitress left, Arlington continued, "The meeting was in his office in the front of the house. Some of the furniture was worn, but it felt like a display, rather than a well-worn room. Both Freddie and DeMarius acted like peers – neither differential to the other. DeMarius was a little famous from when he was a little boy and had called 911 after his mother overdosed."

John said, "I remember him. Cute boy with pleading voice on call."

Arlington continued, "Yes and he wanted to be one of the people in the program. At the time, this didn't make any sense to me. A gang leader leaving for real work? However, his previous notoriety stimulated the media to give this some air time, which really drove the program. In reflection, I think I heard what I wanted to hear, but I probably was being worked over for their agenda."

John Healy, asked "What did you think of these guys?"

Arlington spent a few seconds looking away then said, "As I left there, I was excited. It seemed like a dream come true. Then, I thought about the front window mandate on the block and this kind of altruism about caring for the interest in members of their gang having other options did not really match with the feeling of the meeting and everything I had heard about these guys. And I was afraid of them. They were polite and they are both college graduates, but there was an unstated menacing feeling. I got the feeling that they could get you a cup of coffee or cut your throat with the same feelings afterward."

He stopped to try his donut. "My God, Bo, these should come with a warning. They are beyond delicious. It feels sacrilegious talking about these guys in the same breath as these donuts!" When he finished his mouthful, he stared at the remaining part of the donut, saying, "My goodness."

He looked at both of them, saying, "Now what has this got to do with why we are here. I received a call from your President, Bo. He is not very nice and less subtle. He wanted me to reach out to LAPD and urge them to go slow on any investigation of this explosion that killed your technician. John, I unfortunately did and I think they gave it to another detective. You must be too good at your job. After I did that, I was concerned about a lot of things. Selfishly, if it comes back on 'Bright Lights,' I may be criticized. But then I thought again about my first visit with 'FreMar.' It's their name, like a couple. They are not helping the program and I worry that they may be doing even worse. Your President is working on a merger and doesn't want any bad press at this time. I am pretty sure that is his only motive."

"I'm sorry, John, for messing up your case and I hope it doesn't have further impact, although I can make another call. I hope you guys don't consider me a selfish and naïve politician who doesn't care about the city or the people who live in it."

Bo spoke first. "Ar, that is not what I think," he said, and looked at John. "Me neither. I know of your history and you have done a lot of good in the community."

Bo asked, "Do you have time pressure, Councilman?"

"I do if you keep calling me Councilman," Arlington replied.

Bo smiled and waved at the waitress, "Three more." And no one disagreed.

When the second helping of donuts came, Bo looked at John, and John knew without words what he was asking and nodded his response.

"Ar, like you, we have something we would like to discuss, but we do not want to hear or read about it."

Arlington responded with a half full mouth of donut, "Sure."

Bo gave the background of the explosion, the details of DeMarius being asked for by the original repair call, the call from Freddie to Bo's office and John's recognizing gang members at the address. "We are sure my family was targeted."

"And my son was with them at the time!" John added.

"We are equally sure John's arrival scared the people off. But we don't know what is really going on. Also, not only is John off the case, so am I. But recent events have made us ignore those commands."

"Maybe I can help," Arlington said. "I think I could go visit Freddie and see what's happening. I am sure he sees me as an old man who could do no harm. He would be bolstered from meeting me before where he fooled me outright. I could go to his house tomorrow after 8:00 pm."

BATTLE PLANS ARE PERFECT UNTIL THE FIRST SHOT

Arlington, John and Bo had discussed their plans on how they would move next. Arlington asked only one thing. "Let me go there alone."

After a long discussion, Bo and John said they would. On the way back to Duncan's house, Bo asked John if he thought Arlington should go alone. "Hell, no!" John said. "But we would still be eating donuts if we hadn't agreed."

They used Duncan's office and a map to decide their approach and would leave early to get there.

Gladys and Knight joined them. Gladys wiped her mouth on Bo's jeans. Knight went to John and curled at his feet while he scratched his ears. Duncan joined him and they shared the plan with Arlington. They asked Duncan to stay there and watch everyone. He agreed.

At the same time, Freddie called DeMarius to come over that evening. He needed to talk with him about what was going on. Freddie was determined to find out why DeMarius was skimming. He wanted to find a reason so he could let this go. He now regretted that he had tried to kill DeMarius. As he reflected on it, it was more ego than anything that had caused him to act. He now saw that he had evolved into a gang leader that would never allow disrespect—and the stealing of HIS money was certainly disrespectful. Freddie had never even thought of not being together or showing any sign of disrespect. Freddie could not consider DeMarius anything but his brother, not in any slang definition, but as family. He had let his temper overrule his thinking. He asked DeMarius to come to the house at 8:30. He would quick-kick the Councilman in 15 minutes.

DeMarius was concerned about Freddie. DeMarius was skimming, but he had a higher lifestyle to live up to. Also, he was working, doing real work. Freddie was just directing the efforts of others. Plus, DeMarius liked all the perks of being the "cover" of the program. The drug connection had given him sex any time he wanted it. Living in the neighborhood had curtailed that, because you always needed to be aware of the environment. You could be attacked by another gang, even shot from your own gang or by some fool who wanted to make a name for themselves.

DeMarius got his gun and tucked it in the back of his jeans. He had to be ready if he needed it. He was going to see this little cutie this afternoon, then head over to Freddie's.

As the evening approached, rain had started—the first rain in 7 months. The oil from the road was raised by the water and Southern California drivers were notoriously awful drivers in the rain. Shortly, there were seven different "sig alerts,"(radio-speak for identifying traffic accidents/construction") virtually crippling the LA freeways and many of the key arteries to them. Most people had alternate routes when there were troubles on the roads, but this night, the alternates also had trouble.

Everybody was going to be late.

CRASHING THE PARTY

Freddie was planning on being honest with DeMarius. Then meeting with the Councilman, probably about the 'Bright Lights' jobs program. The Councilman had not said what he wanted to meet with Freddie about. The Councilman was planning on having a private talk about the death of the technician and any conflict with DeMarius. DeMarius was planning on finding out if he was the target of the explosion. John and Bo were planning on covertly backing up the Councilman without his knowing it. All of them didn't know that Bill and Duncan with Gladys and Knight were backing all of them up.

No one was on time.

Freddie turned off all the cameras and sensors while waiting. He nervously pressed the electronic door to his office—opening and closing it, watching the almost immediate response. He liked his grandmother's house, but loved the virtual castle-like protection that the safe room and electronic surveillance equipment provided.

More than once, he was able to hide out when either another gang or one of the more ambitious members of his gang thought they could get at him. He called in others who were well prepared to address the attackers.

However, tonight was just DeMarius and the Councilman, so he nor they didn't need any photographs or videos of their meetings. He left the safe room and closed the electronic door.

Freddie sat at his office desk and he put his gun on a side table. He wanted DeMarius to feel comfortable. He did, however, keep his knife. DeMarius might actually be mad at him, he thought. The doorbell rang.

After Freddie opened the door, DeMarius quickly took off raincoat and hat and laid them on the chair in the entryway. He shivered as Freddie asked him into his office. They sat across from each other and DeMarius took notice of the gun on the side table.

Freddie said, "I didn't want you to be uncomfortable." It had been eight months since DeMarius had been back to the house. They had gone to a Lakers game when DeMarius had gotten the company Lakers tickets six months ago, but had met at the game.

"Why would I be uncomfortable?" asked DeMarius.

"Because I tried to have you killed," Freddie quickly replied.

"Yeah, I figured that was your doing. What were you thinking?"

Freddie smiled. "Because you were stealing our money! And doing your own business on the side."

"I was only a little late."

"Eight months late on a monthly bill?"

"Well, there is that. I am taking it that you don't want to kill me tonight." DeMarius said, looking at the gun.

"No, I actually regret it. I hadn't seen you in months and I kept dealing with the normal crap here in the hood, while you were enjoying the high life. I just missed you."

"And your solution was to blow me up? A little overreaction, huh? And it has brought heat down on our money flow from within the company."

"That was the issue—there was no money flow!" Freddie answered.

"You do know that I actually do work for them. But I wanted a better place to live and it cost a lot more. I didn't think I needed to ask you where I should live." DeMarius held out his hands and raised his eyebrows.

"You do if I'm paying for it."

DeMarius started to get up and Freddie jumped up as well. DeMarius said, "Hold on, I got some money in the raincoat. Let me get it."

Freddie said, "No, let me." He grabbed the coat and pulled out a stack of cash. "How much, DeMarius?"

"About 20 grand or so. I thought I would show some good faith here."

Freddie tossed the money on the table and went around the desk and they both sat down again.

"Why didn't you just tell me what you were doing?" Freddie asked.

"I am a grown man and ought to be able to do what I want without asking anyone for permission. I haven't been down here for a long time and I don't want to come back. My life is a lot more enjoyable in the city—not the inner city."

Freddie felt like he had been slapped. They had been together for almost 20 years and DeMarius was leaving.

"What do you mean exactly?" he asked.

DeMarius sighed, "Look, I will still deal for you AND make my payments, but I am not coming back here again. I live a 'class life' now."

A final insult, Freddie thought.

"I got someone coming to the house shortly. Let me get back to you on this."

"You can do anything you want, but I am through with being here," DeMarius said.

"Let me walk you out."

As Freddie opened the door, they both noticed that the rain had taken a break.

DeMarius walked off the porch and turned, "I'll see you, Freddie."

Freddie said, "Wait up a sec." He walked over and hugged DeMarius. As he did, he felt the gun and it triggered his rage. He pulled out the knife and slit DeMarius's jugular.

Arlington Johnson was walking down the block about four houses down. He noted that the rain had momentarily stopped. He knew about the demands of the neighborhood from Freddie that no cameras or cars were allowed on the block. He had several constituents complain that they were forced to cover all front windows. He reflected that coming alone was a little too bold and wished that he would have asked Bo and/or John to at least back him up. He saw two people on the porch step towards each other and hug. In less than a few seconds, one of them had fallen down.

Across the street, Bo and John were crouching behind some buses and saw Arlington running toward the two men after one of them had fallen. John said, "He should be running the other way. Let's go." Arlington reached DeMarius before Bo and John.

Freddie said, "Your timing is piss poor, Councilman," and reached down and pulled Arlington up.

John and Bo were running at full speed yelling, "Hold it!"

Freddie wrapped his arm around Arlington's neck and pointed the knife at his neck.

"You guys stop right there or I will slit this guy's neck."

Bo kept walking as John took his gun out and pointed it at Freddie saying, "He dies, you die."

Bo noticed the gun tucked in the back behind the belt of the fallen man and moved over to look like he was going to give some comfort.

Freddie turned and yelled at Bo to stay away. John continued to move forward. Freddie was screaming, "I am losing it, man. You guys have to back away or…"

Just then, something black materialized out of the darkness and jumped at Freddie's head. He flinched and turned momentarily, letting go of Arlington. Bo ran and tackled Arlington to get him out of the way. Freddie was also on the ground and quickly jumped to run in the house. He slipped from his shoes being wet in the entryway, then pulled himself into his office, hit the button to the safe room and literally fell into it while simultaneously pressing it to close.

Outside, Bo was checking Arlington for injuries and John was roughly petting Gladys, saying, "Good dog! Good dog!" Duncan had come up quickly after and Gladys went to him.

John went into the house with his gun stretched out in front and turned to look in the office, seeing one foot cut just above the ankle and a leg cut mid-thigh, bleeding out.

It took a while to figure what had happened until John realized that the steel door was an entry to a safe room where not all of Freddie made it.

Duncan was the first to say, "We need to get out of here!" calling for a car to pick them up. Less than a minute later a car came around the corner and parked in front. Duncan got in with Gladys and urged Bo, John and Arlington to follow. Bill started the car moving and asked, "Where would you gentlemen like to go?" like a cab driver. It was a good 30 seconds before they laughed.

Then the questions and the rain began.

"What are you all doing here?" asked Arlington.

"What are you doing here?" Bo asked Duncan.

"Those are not the questions. The question is, 'What are we going to do next? Besides getting out of here?'" Duncan said.

"We should call the police," Arlington offered. It was followed by a chorus of, "No!!!" most emphatically by John, the policeman.

John said, "There is no person who is in harm at the moment."

Arlington said, "What about the two men, Freddie and the other one?"

Bo said "The other one was DeMarius. And was dead on the grass with a bleed-out from being cut in the jugular."

"What about Freddie, then?" the Councilman asked.

John said, "Freddie is no more. He had a safe room he was running toward with a very sharp steel door that cut off one foot at the ankle and midthigh on the other leg. He may have bled out with the thigh wound before I even entered the house. Who besides us knows we were even here? Could neighbors have seen us through their windows or cameras?"

Arlington told them about the rules neighbors were forced to live by.

"What about Freddie's cameras? Bo asked.

Duncan answered, "I know that brand of camera and none had the blue light signifying they were working. Even the gnome camera which had the blue light in his eye was off."

Then John said, "Then this didn't happen tonight. None of us were here. One thing—did everybody turn their phones off?" Everybody nodded.

"I am so glad to be with such criminal minds." He laughed.

"Is everybody okay with never talking about this with anyone or ourselves?" John continued.

Everybody nodded.

John continued, "And, Arlington, the reason for us being here is because you needed us here."

Arlington nodded.

Duncan said, "The same answer for us, Bo."

And Bo nodded.

Bill said, "And I am the driver. Is Anybody else hungry?"

Everybody nodded.

Duncan said, "With Knight here, can we do a drive-through?"

Knight barked.

THREE WEEKS LATER

Not talking about that night was easy, but there were issues that remained "unresolved." Not the least of which was, "Was there a continuing threat to Bo, his family, or anyone connected to Freddie or DeMarius, like Claire in the office and Jenny in the field office?"

Bo, John and Arlington sat in his office to discuss how to approach this, all drinking Dr. Pepper.

"There is new leadership at Freddie's gang," Arlington began. "I could meet with them and discuss this with them."

Bo asked, "Why would they do this?"

Arlington said, "I already reached out to them to discuss the 'Bright Lights' program. They seemed more than willing to meet. There are two of them—Dr. Dredd and Tracer. Who knows their real names? In any event, they moved into the house where Freddie lived. I think they might be looking for a 'friend' in the city government in case they get in trouble."

"That might really work. You are not going there alone," John said firmly.

"Gentlemen, I am never going alone anywhere again except where my mother lives," said Arlington. Everyone laughed, ensuring Arlington would drink another Dr. Pepper after everyone left.

They set the meeting for the next day at 10:00 am. John was the driver and picked up Bo, then Arlington.

John announced, "I looked up the names and each had a sizable rap sheet, but no violence in any of it." He continued, "But these were the two I saw as I drove by coming to your mom's house, Bo."

"Is that going to be an issue?" Bo asked.

"No, I think it can work to our advantage. They do not want to be associated in any way to DeMarius and Freddie. My friend in the Gang Crime Unit tells me that all the gang members were very afraid of both of them because of their volatility and quick anger. They actually like these two guys."

As they arrived, John said to Arlington, "You should lead this conversation, but I hope it is okay if I say a word or two."

"Certainly! Do I introduce you as a Policeman and Bo as a Security Agent?"

"Yes, they'll recognize me from when I recognized them and we can assume they know about Bo. It will establish that we are not trying to trick them."

The door opened as they were walking up the pathway.

"Good morning, Councilman. Who are your friends?" said Tracer.

✝

After the introductions, Tracer led them inside to a seating area that sported a beautiful leather couch and three matching leather chairs. There was a very large TV screen and some decorative paintings with standing lamps around the walls. It looked like an Ethan Allen showroom. Dr. Dredd was waiting and stood up and shook hands with all of them welcoming them to the room. Bo thought, "This seems like a business meeting."

And it was for Tracer and Dr. Dredd. They had their own agenda and it had nothing to do with the 'Bright Lights' program.

John said, "You guys really look familiar. Have we met?"

"I think I would remember meeting you, John," Tracer replied.

Dr. Dredd said, "We get that a lot. We all look alike, you know."

"Not to me, guys." John hesitated a bit, "Maybe I am mistaken."

Everyone knew what they were talking about.

Tracer said as he wanted the subject changed, "Councilman, you wanted to talk about the 'Bright Lights' program?"

"I did, and a number of other things. First of all, there was a credible threat to the families of the telephone company, specifically, Bo Connecticut's family."

Tracer interrupted, "John, are you here in an official capacity as a policeman?"

"No, I am here as a father and a friend. My son also was in some level of danger. It seems there was a break in privacy as Freddie obtained Bo's home address and we were worried that he had wanted to cause some harm. As you may know, there was a technician killed in recent months."

Tracer looked at Dr. Dredd and Dr. Dredd nodded slightly.

"Whether you know it or not and I expect you do, Freddie and

DeMarius were beyond crazy. It didn't surprise anybody that they killed each other or something like it. There were many people who wanted them dead. But you had to get them together or face the wrath of the survivor. If you are going to kill the King (or Kings, in this case), you better not miss."

John Healy felt that these guys were trying to be straightforward, so he offered some non-public information that might further encourage them to speak freely. John said, "The police report doesn't say that they killed each other. It showed that Freddie did kill DeMarius, but that Freddie was killed by a possible malfunction of his security door. It is considered a closed case."

Bo wanted to get clarity on any future threats. "Are you telling us that no one came to the Valley as a threat?" Bo asked.

Tracer spoke. "Theoretically, you could imagine that Freddie would get somebody to do such a thing. It was not healthy to tell him 'NO' at any time. But I can assure you that there is no continuing activity of any sort in the Valley or will there be."

"We are also concerned about 'Bright Lights' members being directed or threatened like Freddie did," Arlington said.

"There will not be anything like that. We only want people in the gang who want to be in the gang. If they want to leave, that's fine with us. We actually think that will ensure our longevity and safety. So, it is in our best interests," Dr. Dredd added.

"You are being very accommodating. Is there something you want?" asked Arlington.

Again, Tracer and Dredd exchanged glances. "This is quite a nice house," Dr. Dredd replied. "It's still in Freddie's grandmother's name. She has moved out of state, but has agreed to lease it to us. It would be expensive and inconvenient to all to have to go through any formal change in ownership. There is no mortgage and Freddie was diligent on paying the taxes. Our plan is the same. It could be helpful to us if someone could assist us in case of any inquiry."

"And you think I might be that someone?" asked Arlington. He also hesitated a bit. Then he said, "I think I could see my way to help, but I have one request."

"What is that?" asked Tracer.

"These neighbors on this block have complained of very restrictive front views, no cars on the street and occasional menace to them. Could that be addressed?"

Dr. Dredd answered, "It is already being addressed. When you parked in front, did you notice other cars on the street? There are only a few people who are not yet believing that there won't be consequences. In addition, we have hired a contractor to address any damage or rehabilitation for the front views of these homes. These people were terrorized enough. We think that the neighbors would be good neighbors without imprisoning them."

"Why are you doing this?" Bo asked,

Tracer answered this one. "Did you ever have a terrible boss? Then he gets replaced by one who is fair and reasonable. You hope that he/she never leaves. We are not any more worried about being shot on this street than any other place. We actually believe that John here would do anything for his family and friends. We are trying to create that here in this neighborhood without the constant threat of violence. John, I am sure you looked us up. We are not violent."

"What about in the Valley?"

"John, you look familiar, too. IF—and I am not saying we were there—we would undoubtedly have been arguing about how to lie to Freddie. We would not have done anything."

Arlington looked at Bo and John and got the smallest of nods from both.

Arlington stood up and shook hands as did everybody else saying "Thank you, gentlemen."

No one spoke as they got in the car to leave. As John started the car and pulled away, he said, "Maybe there is hope for the world."

ANOTHER SUNDAY DINNER

It had been a month since normal life resumed and normal homes were used. Bo had assured all that there was no danger. Even Gloria believed, but only because Bill had agreed. Today was set for a get-together of all the new and old friends.

Win and Duncan began setting up the tables in the late morning. Duncan had rented long tables, as the dinner had become a party with food. The patio was large enough to host 50 people, but there were only 18 planned for this evening.

"Have you met everybody coming tonight?" Duncan asked.

Win thought for a second. "I have not met two of the mothers, Arlington's and Claire's. I really haven't met Claire face-to-face, but I spoke with her on the phone inviting her for tonight. Sweet girl. I only know Jeremy by reputation, although Bo speaks a lot more complimentary about him lately. And Claire speaks of him as her hero, but it sounded more serious than that."

"It seems that a lot of good things have happened from the

terrible recent events," Duncan offered.

Win responded, "A real nice present wrapped in shitty wrapping paper." She continued, "We will need place cards or people won't mix. Except we will put the boys together. Or they will move the place cards."

"A little controlling?" Duncan asked.

"It's a good idea whether you agree or not. Besides, my control needs are immense!"

Many were bringing different parts of the meal. Duncan had ordered a good variety of chips. He was dissuaded about pizza. But he privately ordered one to be delivered for the boys. There were steaks and crab legs in the kitchen. The meat would be cooked on the barbeque and sliced for serving. The crab legs would be steamed in Duncan's restaurant-level stove.

Arlington and Mary Johnson arrived at 4:15 pm. Mary brought a delicious-looking bean dip and Arlington brought a case of Dr. Pepper.

Shortly after, Claire arrived with Jeremy and her mother, Danielle, in tow. Danielle brought three large Tupperware containers with a salad boasting nuts, dried cranberries, and assorted veggies.

Bill Martini, Gloria and Jimmy soon after arrived, with apple pies and vanilla ice cream.

The rest of the party included Katie Fischer, Jenny and her mother, Beverly, and son, Joshua, and the Healy's—John, sister Lorraine and son Robert.

The boys quickly got a soccer ball and played on the driveway in front of the garage. Duncan's property had 10-foot walls surrounding it with a wooden gate at street level at the driveway. Jimmy always thought it made a great soccer half court.

The mothers—Win, Danielle, Mary and Beverly—quickly began to oversee food preparation. As they looked out the window of the kitchen, Danielle said, "Claire has never been so happy. And I can't believe it was a fat white boy who did it! And the poor boy has lost 20 pounds with Claire supervising his eating habits."

"Same with Jenny, I mean the happy part. Except I believe that Bo is part of it, if not all of it," Beverly said.

"That's funny, Arlington also seems happier of late. I think he hasn't had friends for a long time. Politics takes a lot of time and you can never tell who your friend is. Of course, Bo and John may have saved his life, but I know no details."

Win offered, "You are only as happy as your unhappiest child."

All of them laughed and nodded.

⸸

Duncan was being supervised at the barbecue while cooking the steaks, smiling and ignoring any cooking tips.

He said, "You know, guys, this is my house."

John replied, "I just didn't want the steaks burned."

Lorraine, John's sister, said "Don't listen to him, Duncan. He likes his meat still mooing!"

Gloria said, "I think I will join the real chefs in the kitchen," as she walked off.

Lorraine said, "I will join you."

Jenny said, "Me too."

Bill said, "We just need to keep Bo away from food preparation!"

Bo argued, "I may be world class with the microwave."

Katie countered, "I like my food prepared by others, so I eat out as often as possible."

Arlington sighed, "It's like watching a stand-up comedy show!"

Katie then said, "I have some serious news. Pacific Bell is being acquired by SBC, the former Southwestern Baby Bell. It will be announced tomorrow at 10:00 am. Bob Foster keeps calling it a merger, but several executives have already been told to transfer to San Antonio or take a payout and retire."

"Do you think there will be a layoff?" Bill asked.

"Certainly, they do not need the same number of jobs. You don't need two Presidents! But local is king here. You, Bo and I have local jobs. Bo and I provide value to local government and law enforcement. These are built on personal relationships. So, I think we are safe.

Bill, they are not flying a driver out for a VP dinner. You should be safe as well."

Katie continued, "Bob Foster is calling this a merger to anybody who will listen. Pacific Bell was acquired. They bought us. He is a dead man walking. They say if we had not sold then, we were on the verge of missing the dividend. Millions of people have built their retirement on receiving quarterly dividends from stable companies. Missing a dividend makes you an investment pariah. Then, we would have had layoffs. The stock value would have plummeted."

Katie continued, "Remember Betty Fernandez from the President's office, who was to take over from Bo on the investigation," others nodded. "She had a lawyer friend agree to a small fee and approach our lawyers – another friend of Betty's – to offer a $1.75 Million dollar settlement for Terry's death to his widow. Betty had worked the President to believe this would shine favorably on him in the new merged company. Terry Simpson's widow got the check yesterday."

She stopped and said as she was looking at the couple sitting close to each other at the table, "Who are the lovebirds?"

Bo answered. "That's Jeremy and Claire from my security office."

"How do they fit in here?" she asked.

"They have been life savers this year... with their work. I wanted to thank them." Bo answered.

He looked over at them and then to Duncan, John and Bill who were standing behind Katie and were also smiling.

Bo continued, "I would have bet you a thousand dollars a year ago that they wouldn't be here, but I would have been wrong."

John asked Katie, "What do you do, Katie?"

"Oh, you're the cop, right?

"Detective!"

"Sorry, I didn't mean any disrespect. Bo speaks so highly of you, like you are a friend."

"I am."

"So am I. From the third grade on."

"Again. What do you do now?"

"You ARE an investigator!"

"Right now, a frustrated one."

Katie smiled, "I am the External Affairs District Manager for Southern California. I have to deal with politicians all year."

"Thanks, Katie!" Arlington said sarcastically.

"You know, I need to go inside. I am so close to the world record of unintentional insults. I need new victims. I AM sorry, gentlemen."

John asked, "Would you like some wine first, Katie?"

"It might keep me quiet for a little bit." As she followed John to the table with the wine.

Bill said quietly to Bo. "Are we looking at the next ex-Mr. Katie?"

"No, but we may be looking at the next Mrs. Healy!"

Bo walked over to Jeremy and Claire and sat down. "Thanks for coming today, Guys."

Jeremy answered, "Thank YOU for inviting us."

Claire echoed the thought, "It was also nice to invite my mom."

"Well, she was displaced as well as you."

"Mom loves her sister and they had fun like little kids. Jeremy was as concerned about her as he was about the rest of us."

Bo then addressed the secret issue. "I cannot thank you enough for calling me that day," and looking at Jeremy, "All eight times. And, Claire, that was heroic of you to tell Jeremy."

"I was so afraid I needed to talk with somebody. Jeremy was so nice that day and beyond. He was not what I thought he was."

Bo said, "He is different than I thought as well. And, Jeremy, you must have lost 20 pounds!"

"23 pounds!" exclaimed Claire.

Jeremy smiled saying, "No more Oreos. Claire has me on a strict diet… and I have never been happier. Hey Bo, I am sorry I was such a jerk for the last year. I was jealous and wanted to be like you, but didn't know how to do it."

"Well, you are great in an emergency!" Claire reached over and touched Jeremy's arm.

Bo saw both of them looking at each other and thought about his mom's saying—"there is nothing like new love."

Bo said, "Talk to you later, guys." But he was sure they never heard him.

He got up and turned around seeing Bill with Gloria, John and Katie with great big smiles and then saw Jenny walking toward him thinking, "Mom is right." He caught himself smiling at Jenny.

†

After dinner, where everyone had marveled at the food and were clearly enjoying new love and new friendships, Katie grabbed Bo and Bill and asked them to go inside with her.

"When is your wedding with John?" Bill quipped.

"You are not funny, Martini. But he is a good-looking man."

"That's not what I wanted with you guys. I received an email to my office yesterday. I printed it. The heading was to me, but from a weird email address."

Hello Nancy Drew
I think you and the Hardy Boys need to talk.
MG

"Do you know what this is?"

Bill said, "I have no idea."

Bo said, "And things were just settling down. MG is Michael

Gonzales, the CID agent in Iraq that was moved back to the states."

"No, I remember the name was Eric Addley," Bill said.

Bo mentioned, "That was the name given to Katie by the new CID agent. But we knew his name was MG—Michael Gonzales."

"Oh my God, how do you remember all this?" Katie asked.

"I have never forgotten it. Someone wanted us out of the country and not looking at it. This email suggests that the same thing happened to MG. Can you reach him?" Bo asked.

"Most likely through the strange email."

Bo said, "And things were just settling down."

ACKNOWLEDGEMENTS

Thanks to my sister, Patty McGuigan, author of *Leonardo and the Time Travelers* and *Beyond Widow*, for her support, love and persistent encouragement that helped me finish this book.

Thanks to my family – Ann, Mick, Kelly, Molly, Lisa, Cooper and Emma – who have helped me understand the love of family and given meaning and purpose to my life.

Thanks to my editorial team – Maria Mayer Feng and Kate Ryan – who make me sound logical, seem sensible and be a correct speller.